ICE FISHING

THE ULTIMATE GUIDE

WRITTEN AND PHOTOGRAPHED BY
TIM ALLARD

ICE FISHING

THE ULTIMATE GUIDE

WRITTEN AND PHOTOGRAPHED BY
TIM ALLARD

Published by
The Heliconia Press, Inc.
1576 Beachburg Road, Beachburg, Ontario K0J 1C0 Canada
www.helipress.com

Written by: Tim Allard
Edited by: Lori Covington
Photography by: Tim Allard, except as noted.
Design and Layout by: Ken Whiting

Library and Archives Canada Cataloguing in Publication.

Allard, Tim, 1976-
Ice fishing : the ultimate guide / written and photographed by Tim Allard.

ISBN 978-1-896980-49-2

1. Ice fishing. I. Title.

SH455.45.A55 2010   799.12'2   C2010-902553-9

About Safety

Ice fishing is an activity with inherent risks, and this book is designed as a general guide, not a substitute for experience. The publisher and the author do not take responsibility for the use of any of the materials or methods described in this book. By following any of the procedures described within, you do so at your own risk.

CONTENTS

ABOUT THE AUTHOR

Tim Allard is a full-time outdoor journalist. He's a regular contributor to numerous North American publications and is a member of the Outdoor Writers of Canada and the Outdoor Writers Association of America. Always striving to balance accurate reporting, captivating photography, and delivering the straight goods to his readers, Tim's passion for angling spans all seasons, but he's been under ice fishing's spell from a young age. He logs dozens of days on the frozen water each year, snapping both hook sets and photos. Tim lives in Ottawa, Ontario with his wife, Sue.

ACKNOWLEDGEMENTS

Several people were instrumental in this book from its initial conception to the finished product in your hands.

It began with a serendipitous conversation with the book's publisher, Ken Whiting, during a kayak fishing adventure on the Ottawa River. From the get go, Ken's inspired me with a contagious enthusiasm as have the other staff at The Heliconia Press: Brendan Mark, Nicole Whiting and Will Richardson.

Keeping momentum going for this project during a tough economic climate was challenging, but a massive kudos is extended to Chris Leonard of Snosuit (www.snosuit.com), and John Peterson and John Crane of Northland Fishing Tackle (www.northlandtackle.com) for sponsoring this project and keeping myself and a team of anglers outfitted and geared up. Richard Gallace of Baffin boots (www.baffin.com) provided footwear so that our feet stayed warm no matter how far the temperature dropped.

Several other companies provided support and equipment for the book and other writing projects over the years. My appreciation goes to: Brecks / Williams, Frabill, Gamma Technologies, Glacier Glove, JB Lures, Johnson Outdoors / Humminbird, HT Enterprises, Kombi Sports, PowerPro, Lorpen socks, Lindy Fishing Tackle, Versa Electronics / MarCum Technologies, P-Line, Pure Fishing (for Berkley and Trilene products), Rapala Canada (for Sufix, Cortland, Storm, Gamakatsu, Luhr Jensen, Blue Fox, and Normark products), Rose Creek Anglers for their Polar Ice Jig Box, Salmo Lures Canada, Shimano Canada, St. Croix Rods, Seaguar, Stren, StrikeMaster Ice Augers, and Vexilar. Some of the above companies also provided product images used in the book, for which I'm grateful.

One of the best things about ice fishing is the team element and working with other anglers to solve the ever-changing "where are the fish" puzzle. The development of this book is no different. I'm indebted to the following regular hard-core ice adventurers Steve Barnett, Jack Levert, and Rob Jackson (rjnbirdeesoutdooradventures.blogspot.com)

for always being up for a fish, sharing spots and insights, keeping me laughing, and dealing with frozen fingers during photo shoots. I also thank the following angling friends for ongoing annual support: Daryl Allard, Mike Bredlaw, Serge Bricault, Justin Hoffman, Adam Howell, Rick Klatt, Ian Krzyzanowski, Ed Puddephatt (www.paddletales.com), "Big" Jim McLaughlin, Pepe Parisien, Jamie Pistilli, Wally Robins, Derek Samson, Paul Shibata, and Don Theoret.

Jeff "Gussy" Gustafson (www.gussyoutdoors.com) deserves accolades for hosting me and a gang of others on Lake of the Woods in 2009. The trip wouldn't have been a success either without top-notch, ice warriors Davis Viehbeck, guide Dave Bennett (www.wildaccess.ca), and Dean Howard of Campfire Island Camp (www.campfireisland.com).

In addition to my immediate circle of angling amigos listed above, I also sincerely thank the following experts who shared their ice fishing knowledge to help add depth and variety to the content of this book: Brian "Bro" Brosdahl (www.brosguideservice.com), Greg Clusiau (www.fishtec. com), Jacob Edson, Gord Ellis (www.gordellis.com), Dave Genz (www. davegenz.com), Pat J. Kalmerton (www.wolfpackadventures.com), Dustin "Dusty" Minke (www.northcountrymktg.com), Jason Mitchell (www. fishdevilslake.net), Paul Nelson of Bemidji Area Lakes Guide Service (panelson@paulbunyan.net), Gord Pyzer, Noel Vick, and Tom Zenanko (www.icefishingtoday.com).

I also wish to express my thanks to John Blaicher of Blaicher Marketing International Inc. for his expertise and assistance with the Ice Safety Chapter. I'm also grateful to Steven J. Cooke, Ph.D., Associate Professor of Fish Ecology and Conservation Physiology at Carleton University, Cory Suski, Ph.D., Assistant Professor of Natural Resources and Environmental Sciences at the University of Illinois at Urbana, Mark S. Ridgway, Ph.D., Research Scientist with the Ontario Ministry of Natural Resources (OMNR), and Caleb Hasler, Ph.D. Candidate at Carleton University, for sharing their research findings regarding winter biology of many fish, but particularly centrarchids. John M. Casselman Ph.D., Adjunct Professor Queen's University, Department of Biology also provided data on the winter environment and its affect on northern pike and other cool-water fish. OMNR Area Biologist, Scott Smithers, offered valuable information on selective harvest principles and catch and release practices. Jeremy Holden, Fisheries Biologist with the Ontario Federation of Anglers and Hunters, also provided important reference material. I'd also like to note that the "Freshwater Fishes of Canada" by W. B. Scott and E. J. Crossman was used as a reference source for species-specific details in this book.

Outside the fishing world, I owe a huge thanks to long-time friend and professional editor Joe Boulé for his poignant comments on this book. Kudos too to Mike Laidlaw for years of writing collaboration.

Ray and Joyce, thanks for unlimited support and always making your sons a priority. Brother Jeff, I dig that you can find humor in anything. To all three, thanks for being friends as much as family.

Lastly, to my long-time partner and wife, Sue. Your unwavering support, positive attitude, and perma-grin keep me even-keeled on this rollercoaster ride of life.

INTRODUCTION

Ice fishing's a fun and exciting activity. Whether you're a beginner or an expert, a lone wolf angler or a parent with fish-fanatic youngsters, fishing on ice has lots to offer everyone. The hard-water season, as it's affectionately called by ice enthusiasts, provides unique experiences, exhilarating challenges, and plenty of great fishing opportunities. To winter anglers, the ice covering your favorite water body is a pathway to new possibilities and not a barrier.

Ice is the great equalizer. Anglers who were bound to land all summer can now explore beyond the reach of their furthest shoreline cast. Once ice is a safe thickness, mid-lake humps and long, extending points become accessible. Snow machines and all-terrain vehicles let you cover more ground, but even on foot a confident ice angler can experience great fishing whatever the target species.

There's no shortage of species to target beneath the ice either. The icy waters appeal to the temperature preferences of cold-water sport fish, like lake or brook trout, which remain rambunctious in winter. Cool-water fish, such as walleye, pike, and yellow perch, also stay active beneath the ice. Even warm-water species like bluegills need to feed and make good winter game.

Winter also provides unique finesse fishing advantages. Layers of snow help mask your presence overhead and dampen sound. Plus, you can jig lures with the utmost precision. The stationary sheet of ice gives you a fishing edge envied by even the most masterful open-water anglers with exceptional boat control skills. Use a portable sonar and a sensitive rod outfit on the ice and your jigging efficiency grows exponentially.

Ice fishing's a very communal activity too. One of my fondest memories from this past winter was fishing out of an ice house with my wife and another couple. The four of us enjoyed the rustic luxuries of hot dogs prepared on a portable stove, the steady warmth from a propane heater, and infectious tunes sounding from a portable stereo. This was the laid-back, cozy setting for an evening of great crappie fishing filled with laughter and friendly banter about the biggest catch. Better yet, even when my adventures shift from lackadaisical ones to intense fish-hunting forays, the social side of ice angling never wanes. Winter weather or tough fishing never interferes with the joke telling and overall jovial spirit my friends and I take to the ice.

Enhancing the flavor of ice fishing's social spice is that some of the most picturesque and awe-inspiring landscapes occur in winter. My immediate recollection includes scenes of freshly fallen snow on pines lining a remote trout lake and an expanse of bare ice reflecting the golden glow of a sunset. If you've been avoiding ice fishing because of the stereotypical downers courtesy of Old Man Winter, I hope this book inspires you to change and take up fishing on ice.

Now I'll admit, ice fishing isn't always a euphoric trip and it has its own particular set of challenges. After all, you're fishing during winter. Cold temperatures, deep snow, and fish behavior are hurdles to overcome, but they're all surmountable. Especially with the improvements in clothing and gear in recent years, it's never been a better time to ice fish.

In the past decade, outdoor apparel and equipment have become increasingly more refined. The trend is apparent on the community fishing holes as more anglers embrace the latest tools, whether portable sonar units, fast-cutting power augers, or ice-fishing specific outerwear suits. With the addition of new equipment and the ongoing innovation of existing gear, ice anglers are more equipped than ever to not only catch fish, but stay warm and comfortable while doing it.

This book covers everything you need to know about ice fishing. It's an all-encompassing guide and has two main sections. The first outlines the equipment and principles you need to get started. Inside you'll learn about:

- Safety facts, such as safe ice thicknesses, how to test ice and avoid risky areas, and what to do should you or someone else fall through
- Clothing choices from early winter to the season's end
- Rods, reels, line, basic lures and other tackle to catch a variety of sport fish

- Ice augers, including tips on efficient drilling, maintenance, and pros and cons of power and manual models
- Shelters and fish houses from basic wind breaks to sophisticated portable flip-over ice huts
- Portable sonar, GPS units and underwater cameras and how to use these electronics to boost your fishing success

The other section of the book details tactics and strategies to catch winter's most popular sport fish. It describes:

- The environment beneath the ice that affects fish feeding, location, and activity during early, middle, and late winter phases
- Spots on lakes and rivers to find a variety of fish, including: walleye, perch, crappie, bluegills, northern pike, stream trout, lake trout, whitefish, and more
- The hottest lures available, along with bait tipping and modification tricks to catch your favorite fish through the ice
- Jigging secrets – from the basic foundations of this vertical presentation to advanced tactics that fool fish to bite
- Setline rigging methods and fishing strategies for dead-sticks and tip-ups
- "Ice Angling Essentials" - a series of techniques guaranteed to improve your angling strategies and make you a better ice angler
- Pro tips from some of North America's finest ice anglers and guides
- Conservation and responsible angling practices, such as fish handling methods and selective harvest principles

Ultimately, this book covers everything you need to know to get geared up and catch a variety of sport fish through the ice. I have complete confidence it'll be informative on your first read and also remain a reference material for many winters to come.

CLOTHING

Using a Layering System
Keeping Your Extremeties Warm and Dry
Protecting Yourself from the Sun

CLOTHING

It's critical that you stay warm and dry when ice fishing; not only for your comfort, but for your health and safety. Being cold also impacts your ability to fish effectively. It's tough to concentrate and finesse jig a fussy panfish with freezing fingers. This chapter is about clothing and recommendations on how to dress appropriately. The right type of clothing, materials, and layering practices will keep you toasty when temperatures fall below freezing.

On several outings, I've been completely exposed without the comfort of a shelter and was battered by steady winds in bitterly cold temperatures. But dressed with plenty of layers and an insulated ice fishing suit, I didn't get chilled. At the other end of the spectrum, I've had fantastic late-ice adventures walking in several inches of slush (and over a foot of safe, solid black ice) under a warm sun. In conditions like that, insulated rubber boots and sunscreen were the two most critical things I needed to stay comfortable.

My goal in this chapter is to make sure you know what you need to stay warm and dry throughout the hard-water season. I'll describe different outerwear options, from insulated ice fishing jackets and bib pants to flotation suits, and talk about proper layering underneath them. Once we've got your core body covered, I'll review what to look for in boots, hats, and gloves and mitts to keep your extremities dry, and how to protect yourself from the sun. I want you to be ready for the coldest temperatures: I'm talking about those days when you're reaching regularly for the skimmer to clear out a freezing ice hole, but toughing out the cold because you're icing plenty of fish.

USING A LAYERING SYSTEM

Odds are that you already know about the importance of layering clothing, so this section might just be a helpful review. However, if you're new to the idea, let me assure you layering clothing effectively is the best way to stay warm and comfortable in winter conditions.

Layering involves wearing a combination of clothes to regulate your body temperature so that you don't overheat or get cold. Yes, you can overheat in winter. Carrying a 25-pound auger, punching one hole after another through the ice or pulling a portable shelter while trudging through calf-high snow constitutes more than enough exertion to boost your body temperature. (This is also why I often drill holes and move if I feel cold. It's the perfect warm-me-up routine, with the added benefit of keeping me mobile and searching for fish.)

If you're overdressed for the more active moments in ice fishing, you'll get too hot and kick up a sweat. This is a problem when you're not properly dressed as sweat-soaked clothes against your skin can quickly cause you to get chilled once your activity level drops. If you sweat while wearing the right layers, however, most of your perspiration will be wicked away from your skin, leaving you relatively dry while still warm and comfortable. When possible, it's best to avoid excessive sweating by shedding insulating layers when you know you'll be active, and putting them back on when you stop so you don't lose too much body heat.

Layering clothing keeps you comfortable. Insulated Snosuit Bibs and a fleece hoodie were all Rob Jackson needed on a calm and mild March outing.

Your layering system must work for the climate conditions (e.g., temperature and wind chill), your activity level, and your individual thermostat or personal tendencies. Layers can be divided into three categories: base, mid, and outer. These layers act in unison to block wind, repel water, trap heat, wick moisture away from your body, and allow your skin to breathe. Individually every layer performs specific functions, so let's look at each in detail.

Base Layer

The base or inner layer is the first level of clothing you wear. It's what goes against your skin. Long-sleeved tops and full-length bottoms are examples of inner layers and are often made of synthetic material like polyester or natural materials such as silk or wool.

The base layer should fit snugly, but not so tight that you feel constricted. A cozy fit ensures the materials stay in contact with your skin and wick away moisture to keep you feeling warm and dry; if your clothing is too loose, this won't happen.

When shopping for inner layers, you'll find that they're often classified in three weight types: lightweight, mid-weight, and heavyweight. Garments classified as lightweight are usually designed for high-aerobic activities where moisture wicking is crucial to comfort but provide little insulation. Mid-weight base layers (often called long underwear) provide moisture-wicking properties and some insulation. A heavyweight layer wicks moisture but is also intended to provide significant insulation in very cold conditions or for more sedentary activities.

So what does this mean on the ice? Your base layer isn't likely to change much throughout the ice season because it's easy to adjust insulation using the other two layers. I recommend wearing a lightweight, long-sleeve polyester or merino wool shirt, sometimes adding a mid-weight one on top of this if it's extremely cold out. For bottoms, a set of mid-weight long underwear made of the same materials above will serve you well. There are a variety of sock options, but I'll discuss how to dress and keep your feet warm later in this chapter.

Middle Layer

The middle layer provides insulation. It should be a loose fit, but not baggy since it needs to maintain contact with the inner layer to function properly. Middle layers are made from a variety of materials. Common ones are fleece, polyester, and merino wool. Many manufacturers produce patented synthetics, such as PrimaLoft® or Thinsulate™, and natural blended materials for middle layers as well. These will trap your body heat in the small air pockets designed into the fabric. In addition to thermal padding, middle layers also help move moisture away from the base layer towards the outer layer. Expect to see lightweight, mid-weight, or heavyweight descriptors for middle layers.

Except for the balmiest ice fishing weather, you'll likely want to wear more than one middle layer. Here's how I use middle layers for different weather conditions and ice fishing scenarios. On my upper body my base layer starts with one or two lightweight polyester long-sleeved shirts for wicking. Next, I add either a mid-weight polyester shirt or light- to mid-weight fleece. In colder weather, I'm often dressed with both. I may also wear a fleece vest. Relatively inexpensive and light, a fleece vest provides added insulation and I bring it whenever I head out on the ice. In extremely cold weather I also pack a heavyweight fleece or a light-weight, synthetic-filled jacket.

On my lower body I have a few options. I wear a pair of heavy-weight fleece pants when I'm heading out in extremely cold temperatures. Another option is a pair of polyester or nylon-mix pants which can be worn over mid- or heavyweight underwear for extra warmth.

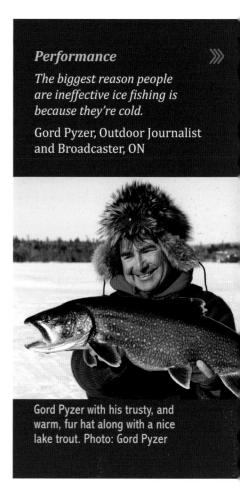

Gord Pyzer with his trusty, and warm, fur hat along with a nice lake trout. Photo: Gord Pyzer

Brendan Mark and Tim Allard gear up for a day on the ice.

Mid-layer clothing often has extra features to increase your comfort and the garment's functionality. Keep this in mind for ice fishing. Underarm zippers and zip-up collars allow you to ventilate easily and regulate your temperature without having to frequently remove or add layers. Drawstrings at the base of shirts and jackets help trap in heat when closed tightly or can be loosened for air flow if you get too warm. On mid-weight shirts, look for cuts long enough to cover your torso so that they'll stay tucked-in when leaning over or reaching. When it comes to mid-weight jackets, opt for ones with wind-blocking properties. This lets you use the jacket occasionally as an outer layer, when conditions allow. Zippered leg bottoms are also handy for getting layers on and off, and create a snug fit when closed.

Outer Layer

The outer layer is your final line of defense against winter's elements, blocking wind and repelling rain and snow. It's also the last membrane that moves moisture away from the body. Several options exist in non-insulated and insulated garments.

Non-Insulated Outer Layers

The most common types of non-insulated outer layers used in ice fishing are high-end rain suits and shell jackets. When combined with an adequate base of middle insulating layers, these outer shells can be comfortable in mild temperatures. This type of set-up tends to be preferred by those whose angling activities involve lots of walking and hand-drilling of holes or for those who venture out when temperatures aren't cold.

The main downside to non-insulated outerwear is that you need to be prepared with extra mid-layers in case the temperature drops. Depending on the fit, it can be challenging to pack enough layers underneath this outerwear to stay both warm and comfortable in cold conditions. I mainly stick to non-insulated outerwear when I'm hiking in to remote back lakes or in extremely mild conditions.

Insulated Outer Layers

Insulated outerwear not only blocks wind, rain and snow, but also provides another layer of warmth, making it perfect for fishing long hours without the protection of a hut. I wear these about 95% of the time be-

A warm mid-layer combined with non-insulated outerwear kept Daryl Allard comfortable in unseasonably warm temperatures during a late-ice yellow perch outing.

cause I'd rather have to take layers off and keep fishing than head home early because I'm too cold.

Recently, I took out some friends new to ice fishing. It was nasty out. Strong gusts made for a steady wind-chill that relentlessly ripped down the river we were fishing. Luckily I was able to outfit them each with a jacket and pair of bibs from Snosuit and warm boots that kept them cozy all day. Half way through the outing, my friend said, "I can't believe how warm I am out here. I would have never thought I'd have lasted this long when I looked at the weather this morning." This is the benefit of quality ice-fishing outerwear. Not only does it keep you comfortable, but it gives you the confidence you'll stay warm and can fish hard in the worst winter weather.

There's lots of apparel to choose from. Winter hunting outerwear or snow machine clothing makes a great cross-over to ice fishing because they're designed to perform in cold-weather conditions. High-end winter jackets and pants can also provide adequate insulation and protection from the elements. Despite these options, many anglers are converting to ice-fishing specific suits. Snosuit Performance Winterwear Jacket and Bibs, Clam Corporation Ice Armor, Vexilar Cold-Snap Gear, StrikeMaster HardWater Wear, and Innovative Design Arctic Armor Suit are examples of suits on the market.

The great thing about a jacket and bibs is you can shed layers when you get warm.

Snosuit's Bibs and Jacket provide the ultimate in warmth, comfort, and reliability so you can focus on fishing.

Plenty of pockets are a must in outerwear. They let you carry fishing essentials - like this tackle box - when hole-hopping.

Look past the walleye in Adam Howell's hands for a sample of a one-piece flotation suit.

Important Outerwear Features for Ice Fishing

Let's look at outerwear design in more detail, since there are several features to take into account to improve your on-ice comfort and fishing efficiency. In jackets and pants, you'll want plenty of exterior pockets that won't affect the fit of the garment as you load them up with items, like tackle trays. I like deep, over-sized, lined pockets so I can hide my occasionally bare hands from the wind and cold. Internal pockets are handy too for things like cellular phones, wallets, and bait containers.

When it comes to jacket styles, avoid bomber cuts. Instead opt for a jacket that will keep your lower back (and butt) protected at all times, especially when you're seated or leaning forward. Hoods will keep your head and hat dry in snow, sleet, and rain, and block the wind. Look for jackets that have adjustment cords along the collar and waist so that you can tighten them to trap in heat or loosen them for ventilation.

Standard pants are fine on the ice, but bibs are better. Bib pants deliver plenty of coverage that regular ones don't provide, especially when leaning over. They might not be critical on mild winter days, but when it's frigid you'll love the extra insulation they offer. When buying bibs, you should look for adjustable, elasticized shoulder straps to ensure a good fit. Opt for suspenders with an "X" or "H" design to prevent them from slipping off your shoulders. Bibs with cushioning in the knees and the seat are two other features common in ice fishing bottoms. The extra padding makes long hours in a portable hut or kneeling on ice to land a fish more comfortable. Zipper leg openings with sealable flaps make quick work of getting pants on and off over bulky winter boots, (which is a big benefit when you're quickly dressing beside a snow bank in freezing temperatures). Internal boot gators ensure a proper fit while preventing snow from sneaking up pant legs.

Also keep sizing in mind. Adding layers can make jackets that usually fit you a bit too snug. If you're planning on buying an ice suit or other insulating garments for hard-water angling, try them on with several layers and don't be afraid to buy a larger size. For a comfortable and more ergonomic fit, look for articulated elbows and knees. These pleated designs encourage movement without sacrificing fit. Reinforced construction in high-wear areas, such as the seat and knees, are another benefit to ice fishing suits.

One- and Two-Piece Flotation Suits

Flotation suits are another outerwear option, but are in a class of their own. Because it's always best to approach on-ice travel with caution, several winter anglers wear these garments for extra assurance in terms of flotation and thermal protection, especially in areas where ice thickness and safety are uncertain. Anglers have the option of purchasing a one-piece suit or combining jacket and pant models. Some manufacturers of these suits include Mustang Survival and Helly Hansen.

Flotation suits are extremely durable and perfect for the rigors of ice fishing. The suits provide an excellent defense against inclement weather and their insulating foam keeps you warm. In addition to delivering protection above ice, the main purpose of these outfits is to prolong your survival time should you fall into cold water by helping you stay afloat and keeping you warm.

If you decide to buy one, make sure it's approved by the United States or Canadian Coast Guard and meets flotation requirements for your weight. Once these criteria are met, try it on with all the layers you intend to wear to ensure it fits. Be sure to move around in it and test the range of motion for sitting down, walking, and drilling holes. Remember, if the fit isn't comfortable, you're less likely to wear it, defeating the whole purpose of buying one.

One-piece models come in so-called "standard proportions," which means that if you have a longer torso or legs then it can be challenging to get a decent fit. In this case a three-quarter length flotation coat combined with a matching bib pant is a great alternative. Two-piece flotation suits offer increased versatility, letting you wear the jacket or pants alone or together, which is useful to prevent overheating once you arrive at a fishing spot and are confident that the ice beneath you is safe. Just remember that the less body coverage the suit offers, the less thermal protection it gives.

KEEPING YOUR EXTREMITIES WARM AND DRY

With your core body properly covered, all that's left to dress before hitting the ice are your extremities. Hands, feet, and the head (particularly the ears) are often the first things to get cold. The good news is there's lots of gear to ensure you stay toasty from the tips of your toes to the edges of your ears.

How Flotation Suits Work ≫

If you fall through the ice (see Chapter 6 for ice safety details), flotation suits keep your head above water and have buoyant insulation strategically placed to keep you in a horizontal, swimmer's position that will give you the best chance for a self-rescue. The product's insulation does several things. During the initial dunking, the insulation's full-body coverage can help reduce the effects of cold shock, which is the body's immediate distress reaction to cold water. (Cold shock usually starts with a large involuntary gasp followed by a hyperventilation effect, increased heart rate, and panic.) The thermal protection of flotation suits also traps precious body heat until you can get to safety, and helps to fight the onset of hypothermia.

Hands

Keeping your hands warm is a constant challenge when ice fishing, but far from an impossible one with a quality pair of gloves or mitts. Gloves are often preferred for fishing tasks like reeling, jigging, starting augers, or assembling portable shelters. Mitts however, keep fingers together and warmer, making them the top choice for long-distance hauls on recreational vehicles or in extreme cold.

Consider the nuances of ice fishing's activities when choosing a pair of gloves or mitts. They'll need to withstand plenty of abuse over the season. Quality mitts and gloves will feature water-resistant or waterproof materials, plenty of insulation, and rugged construction. High and wide cuffs will provide protection from water and snow, but will also make them easier to put on with cold, cramped fingers.

In the protection of an ice hut or on mild winter days, heavily insulated gloves and mitts will feel like overkill. For these conditions, consider a pair of neoprene gloves, which usually keep hands warm even after gloves become saturated with moisture. Some models feature slits in the thumb and forefinger that improves dexterity and makes easy work of tying knots or using scissors to cut line. Windproof, fingerless or flip-mitts made of fleece with lined neoprene palms are other good options. Regardless of what you choose, carry extra pairs of gloves or mitts on your outings to be prepared in case the ones you're wearing become wet and cold.

Quality gloves, like this Kombi pair that Brendan Mark is using, are invaluable. They feature water-resistant materials, lots of insulation, and durable construction.

Glacier Glove's Premium Fleece Flip Mitt is perfect for mild conditions when having exposed fingers makes everything easier, from baiting lures to jigging rods.

Feet

Keeping your feet warm is of utmost importance on the ice. Once your feet go from chilled to downright cold, it's a challenge to warm them again. It's best to practice prevention and keep them toasty from the start with properly fitting, quality socks and boots.

Whenever I think of cold feet ice fishing I remember an episode during the early dating years with Sue, now my wife. I thought introducing Sue to ice fishing would be a good next step in our budding relationship, so I took her out for an evening. I selected a point that usually produces a few decent walleye as our sunset destination. We arrived, got dressed in outerwear, loaded the flip-up shelter with gear and headed to the spot. I had strategically chosen a short walk, only about 5 minutes from the road. I set Sue up in the hut drilled her a hole, gave her the flasher and my go-to spoon, along with a few jigging tips. She was excited to catch a fish. I grabbed the auger and punched about 10 other holes along the structure. I put out two set-lines and by the time I cleared the holes and returned to the shelter 10 minutes later, Sue looked up and sadly said, "My feet are

Fish Towels

Carry a small towel to dry your hands after handling fish. Fish towels, often used in boats, are ideal for this. Use their straps or clips to attach them to your jacket or inside your shelter so they're always within reach.

Sue Butchart's feet stay well-insulated thanks to a pair of Baffin boots.

getting cold." I knew right then it was game over. It was my fault too for not checking the of boots she had, which were more for "urban winter trekking" than ice fishing. We left the ice and grabbed hot chocolate on the way home. Since then Sue's got a quality pair of ice fishing boots. We now enjoy a few outings a year and still occasionally laugh about this episode.

Socks

The same rule that applies for all your winter clothing holds true here: no cotton. Stick to materials (like wool and synthetics) that will wick moisture away and insulate well even when they get a little damp. In most socks, wool is the main ingredient, but companies have removed the itch factor, eliminated the danger of shrinkage, and have delivered quality products at reasonable prices. Over the past several years I've been impressed with the variety of hiking, crew, and hunting socks on the market. These are available in various thicknesses from light to heavy; arm yourself with an assortment of socks so that you can dress for different conditions.

Some people like to layer socks using a thin to lightweight liner that will move moisture away from the skin, and a second sock made of thicker material to insulate. Layering socks helps keep your feet warm and dry, and can also prevent chafing and blisters. If you decide to wear two pairs of socks, they should fit comfortably. Cramming two similarly-sized socks on top of each other can mean a tight fit. This will constrict your feet and reduce blood flow—a surefire way to get cold toes fast on the ice. Make sure you use a larger-sized outer sock when doubling-up.

Boots

An excellent pair of boots is an absolute must when ice fishing. Any boot you choose should be waterproof to your ankle, and well-made with durable material, but without sacrificing insulation. Your ice fishing boots need to protect you from the elements and keep your feet warm and dry as you drill holes and move around in different conditions. Remember that you get what you pay for; when it comes to boots, go for high quality. Also, as a general rule avoid boots with steel toes or shanks.

Many boot manufacturers will list temperature ratings with their footwear. This ranking allows you to compare one boot to another in terms of insulation provided. It's fundamental to note these ratings are only guidelines. How warm your feet will be is based on your activity level, how much you perspire, your exposure time, the outside temperature, how good your circulation is, and other factors. Personally, I'm prone to getting cold feet and wear a pair of boots rated for -148°F (-100°C). Even though I'll never be exposed to this extremely low temperature, I'm confident my feet will stay warm. Frozen toes will ruin a fishing trip.

In boots rated for very low temperatures, there are two main options that are suitable for ice fishing. The first have a waterproof base and rubber outsole that attach to heavy-duty nylon or leather uppers that go to at least calf level, with laces or buckles that allow you to adjust the fit. The boot liners provide plenty of insulation (the thicker the better) and also wick moisture away from the feet.

The second main option for boots are ones mainly designed for winter or foul-weather hunting. They provide plenty of insulation and contain breathable membranes to allow sweat to escape. High-end models are 100% waterproof. They feature plenty of laces and offer a more streamlined fit to help keep you comfortable for miles of walking. These boots perform well on the ice, provided you've purchased a pair with enough insulation. Some outdoor enthusiasts who are avid hunters as well as ice anglers prefer these boots since both activities are supported with one pair.

During mild spells and in the last weeks of winter, surface water and slush can form on the ice. Once this gets over a few inches deep, I switch to a pair of insulated rubber boots. They provide excellent water protection as well as plenty of thermal padding. Although many reserve these boots exclusively for wet, sloppy conditions I do know a few anglers with furnaces for feet that wear them year round.

A Tip for Toasty Toes »

Pay attention to the distance between your feet and the outsole: The more space, the more protection the boots offer from the cold ground. If you're a few inches taller wearing your ice fishing boots, that's a good thing.

Baffin's fastening buckles make a snug fit a snap even with gloves on.

FIVE RULES FOR WARM FEET

1. Minimize the amount your feet sweat before stepping on the ice. For example, I avoid wearing my ice fishing boots while driving to my destination. Even with the heat on low, your feet can quickly overheat in an automobile. Instead, wear another pair of footwear and then change into your ice fishing boots once you arrive at your destination.

Baffin's Trapper insulated premium rubber boot.

2. Always pack an extra pair of heavy socks and change into them if the ones you are wearing become damp. I also know of anglers who dust their feet with talcum powder to reduce moisture build-up.

3. If you can, upgrade the thickness of your boot insoles for extra insulation and padding. This can sometimes make boots fit a bit better. Replace worn insoles as necessary.

4. Always dry your inserts and insoles after each trip. If you forget and end up heading out on an impromptu outing, you'll probably find that your feet get cold faster than the previous trip because of the damp liners. As far as drying goes, follow the boot's care and maintenance instructions. Some liners can be tossed in a dryer while others must be hung to dry. Boot dryers are also very handy.

5. Finally, prevent ice from forming on your boots; it works against you, sucking heat out from your footwear. Sometimes this can't be avoided, but remove build-up from the toe box as soon as you can.

Good gear kept ice fishing hot sticks Davis Viehbeck (left) and Jeff "Gussy" Gustafson on the water despite nasty conditions. Good thing too, because the lake trout were biting.

Head and Neck

You'll want a few items to protect your head and neck. Start with a warm hat made of wool, acrylic, or fleece. Having different styles, from lightweight to heavyweight, will ensure that you're ready for any degree of weather throughout the ice season. If you choose fleece, look for hats with wind-blocking liners; otherwise wind will blow right through and steal your body heat.

In terms of hat design, short ones like beanies can be great for mild weather, but in cold weather opt for longer stocking hats with adjustable roll cuffs. The cuff lets you cinch the hat further down on your neck and completely cover your ears.

There are a variety of other hats and caps that you can also use for ice fishing. Some ice anglers prefer a "bomber" style for their excellent insulation and flap-down ears. Insulated ball caps with flaps can keep ears warm while shading eyes in sunny conditions. On mild days, you can sometimes get by with a regular ball cap but always bring an insulated hat for back-up in case the weather changes or you start to get cold.

Neck warmers or neck gaiters are more compact and less likely to get tangled than a scarf. They're great for keeping your neck, throat, and even cheeks warm. If you plan to fish in windy conditions or travel on a snow machine or ATV, get a high-end neck warmer designed to block wind.

To protect even more of your face in cold weather, consider a balaclava. Fleece ones can be worn over hats and under hoods, whereas thinner liner-type ones are great for layering under a helmet or hat. Some balaclavas and insulated face masks have ventilation at the nose and mouth so that you can exhale without dampening the material or fogging up glasses.

PROTECTING YOURSELF FROM THE SUN

It's a funny thing: ice anglers spend so much time gearing up to fight the cold that they often overlook the dangers of sun exposure. The fact is you should protect yourself from the sun in the winter as much as in the summer. Snow can reflect up to 85% of UV rays, so you're getting hit from above as well as below by this harmful radiation.

Apply sunscreen with an SPF of at least 30 to your face, neck, ears, and hands roughly 30 minutes before you go outside. Face-specific sunscreens are available, eliminating the greasy feeling of some products. I

Don't Forget! »

Sunscreen is so easy to forget once you get out on the ice. I find the best thing to do is put it on first thing in the morning before you leave the house. Don't forget to reapply throughout the day though.

Greg Clusiau, Ice Fishing Guide, MN

A pair of Oakley sunglasses with polarized lenses keep the author comfortable during bright, late-ice conditions. Photo: Serge Bricault.

prefer a sweat-proof sun block, but I still reapply it frequently throughout the day.

Bring lip balm with an SPF rating of 30 or higher to keep lips from getting sunburned or chapped in the dry winter air. I buy a couple of sticks and tuck them in the inside pockets of my ice jackets before the start of the season so that they're always within reach.

Finally, always take sunglasses on your ice adventures. First and foremost, high-quality sunglasses will protect your eyes from UV rays whenever you're outside. They'll also offer wind protection, reducing watery eyes and increasing your on-ice comfort. Get ones made of sturdy plastic or other composites and avoid metal frames that will just get cold and uncomfortable in winter conditions. I'm also a fan of polarized lenses that help cut down glare and the intensity of light reflected off the snow. They'll also serve you well in the summer, helping you spot underwater structures on open-water outings.

Seriously consider getting sunglasses that offer impact protection as well. It might seem farfetched to think about shielding your eyes from projectiles on the ice, but this past season alone I had some close calls, and I'm not particularly accident-prone. One incident happened at late ice with a friend enjoying some amazing action, hooking plenty of black crappie. My friend, a well-seasoned ice angler, had hooked a slab and hollered to me for help to land the fish. As I started to crouch down toward the hole, the fish came unbuttoned. My friend's bent rod unloaded, sending the tiny ice jig whizzing past my head. Luckily the lure missed me completely, but if it had been a few inches closer, I would have been hit in the face. Fortunately my eyes were protected because I was wearing sunglasses.

Wrap Up

Now that you've got your ice fishing clothing assembled, you're almost ready to hit the ice. The next step is to get the necessary equipment and tackle. To the angling armory...

GEAR & TACKLE

GEAR & TACKLE

When people who don't fish look in on the world of ardent anglers, our tendency to amass hordes of fishing equipment may seem comical, even obsessive. Luckily, many of us have understanding spouses who tolerate garages and basements filled with rods, tackle trays, tip-ups, shelters, electronics, augers, and plenty of cold-weather clothing. Although we may be gear junkies, having the proper equipment is important if you want to catch fish. You need the right tools to do the job well.

If you're a newcomer to ice fishing, don't be intimidated by the copious amounts of products in tackle shops. You only need the basic items to get started and the initial financial outlay doesn't have to be substantial. However, as you become more skilled, expand the number of species you target and increase the techniques you use, you'll want to build your gear selection to include specialized items for specific presentations.

Over the next several chapters, I'll be discussing ice fishing equipment in more detail. This chapter focuses on rods, reels, tip-ups, ice fishing line, lures and baits, terminal tackle, and other useful tools. I'll also explain the nuances of their different applications.

RODS

Using a rod to jig a bait is the mainstay of many ice fishing presentations. Several companies produce rods (and reels) specifically for ice fishing, including: Northland, Berkley Fishing, Frabill, HT Enterprises, Jason Mitchell Elite Series Rods, Nature Vision, Rapala, Shakespeare Fishing Tackle, St. Croix Rods, Storm, Thorne Bros., and Clam Corporation.

My rod-carrying tactics on the ice don't change much from my open-water fishing strategies. I carry several rods so I can employ a variety of presentations. Switching lures is as easy as putting down one stick and grabbing another pre-rigged one. It's also not uncommon to fish for a variety of species in one outing on either the same lake or moving to another partway through the day.

Ice rods should be chosen based on the lures you intend to use and

>> *A Place for Everything*

When I go ice fishing, much like fishing in my boat in the summer, every thing I own has a place, and I know when I put them in that place that they're going to be safe and not get beat up - I want to be 'fishing not fixing!'

Dustin "Dusty" Minke, Hard-Core Ice Angler, MN

the fish you plan to target. Depending on the number of species you want to fish for during the winter, you could get by with one to three rods. The number you purchase and carry beyond three depends on the degree of specialization you would like to integrate into your angling tactics. On most outings, I find myself carrying five rods. This gives me a bit of duplication, but this way I'm prepared for anything.

Let's review rod characteristics. They're important to note because choosing the right ice fishing rod is a prerequisite for your success on the ice.

Choosing an Ice Rod

There are a variety of factors to consider when selecting a rod. The first things to decide on are rod power, action, and length. Once these are established, you can then examine the finer details in rod design such as blank materials, handle styles, and line guides.

Power is Primary

Power describes the strength of the rod blank. Ultra-light, light, medium, and heavy are the main classifications with in-between options like medium-light and medium-heavy being common. What power you select is best determined by your target species and the weight of lure and line that you intend to use.

A quality rod is a must for properly jigging lures, feeling hits, and battling fish.

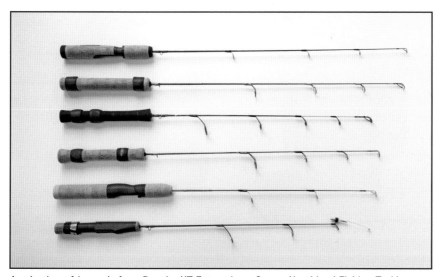

A selection of ice rods from Rapala, HT Enterprises, Storm, Northland Fishing Tackle, Berkley, and St. Croix.

The selection process begins by matching power to the target species that you're after, just as it does when you're picking a rod for open-water fishing. Ultra-light and light rods are good choices for sunfish, small crappie, perch, and small trout. Medium-light to medium rods are recommended for jumbo perch, larger trout, walleye, and whitefish. Medium-heavy to heavy rods are best for pike, lake trout, and trophy walleye. Keep in mind that these are just guidelines to give you a starting point in selecting a stick – I've landed big walleye with a light power rod and finessed jumbo perch with an ultra-light.

If prescreening by species is the first consideration to choosing rod power, determining how you're going to use them is the next important step. If you've had help from salespeople when purchasing rods, you've likely been asked questions about your target species and applications: "What species are you after?" and "What lures do you want to fish with the rod?" The same apply to ice rods.

As an example, if you're presenting a tiny jig to a bluegill on 2-pound test line, an ultra-light rod is the best option. The rod's blank will be balanced with the line and lure's weight. The set-up will be sensitive enough to transmit the subtle vibration of the jig as you work it with the rod, and let you feel when a fish takes the bait. If you were trying to accomplish

Tim Allard's medium-power rod gets a work-out courtesy of a northern pike as Davis Viehbeck waits to help land the fish. Photo: In-Fisherman Magazine.

this same presentation with a medium power rod, you would lose most – if not all – of the rod's sensitivity to feel the lure and bites. At the other end of the spectrum, when using heavy 3/4-ounce spoons to jig aggressively for lake trout or trophy walleye, you need a medium-heavy to heavy power rod to handle the weight of the bait and battle a big fish. Too light a blank and you'll find jigging the bait will become tiring because the rod will bend significantly under the lure's weight with every jigging snap.

If you consider the average weight of the target species you're after and the line and lure weight you plan to fish, choosing rod power becomes a relatively easy decision. Also making this decision-process easier is some rods are designed and marketed for specialized presentations. Long, soft-tipped dead-stick rods or extremely short ones for sight fishing are just two examples of technique-specific sticks. Buying several rods in varying powers ensures you can fish a mix of weighted baits for several fish species. The next two factors to consider are rod action and length.

Understanding Action

Action refers to where the rod flexes along the blank and impacts how you can present lures and play fish.

Fast and extra-fast action rods flex mainly at the tip, medium action rods flex to the middle of the blank, and slow action rods bend from the tip to the bottom of the handle. Extra-fast and fast action rods have limber tips to signal light hits, while the rest of the blank bends little, providing strength. This also ensures solid hook sets. These actions are top choices among most ice anglers when jigging.

Remember my example about using an under-powered rod to work heavy baits? Action can also impact your efficiency. Extra-fast and fast action rods make jigging easier, especially with heavy lures. The stiffer blanks transmit your arm and wrist movements without dampening them. If you try jigging heavy lures with medium-action rods, you'll find that they absorb some of the energy and that you'll need to work harder to jig a bait. Odds are that if you have a few rods in your carrying case, you have a mix of extra-fast and fast action sticks.

Medium action rods perform well when dead-sticking (a tactic of rigging minnows or other bait on hooks or jigs and suspending them without active jigging). A dead-sticking rod features an extremely soft tip to signal a bite and its easy-bending upper blank gives little resistance to a fish when it initially takes the bait.

Testing rod action and power are easy. Take the rod handle in one hand and the tip in the other, and lightly bend the rod to see its action. If you know what kind of action you're looking for, you can quickly try several rods to narrow down your choices. Doing this test also emphasizes the benefits of different lengths of each blank, the next major consideration when buying a rod.

Rod Length

The length you choose depends on your intended style of fishing and a handful of other factors. Longer rods take up more line when lifted and give anglers increased leverage when fighting fish; this makes them suitable choices for handling big catches such as pike and lake trout, or for use in deeper water situations. Longer rods also tend to be more forgiving, absorbing headshakes and hard hook sets along the entire blank. The downside to longer rods is that they can be difficult to use in the closed quarters of an ice hut. The layout of some one-person huts makes it tough to use rods over 28-inches, but the same rod length could easily be used in a roomier shanty or outside a shelter.

Short rods provide less shock absorption. However, they're easier to use in cramped quarters. They're also perfect for sight fishing. Their shortness lets you get close enough to peer down the hole and still effectively work lures. Also, because they move less line when lifted or lowered than longer rods, shorter sticks are better for finesse fishing with subtle jigging moves. If fishing's a family affair, keep in mind that short rods are easier for children to use and can turn pint-sized scraps with sunfish into epic battles.

Once you've narrowed down rod models based on power, action and rod length, you can scrutinize the finer details of rod design.

Blank Materials: A Word on Graphite versus Fiberglass

Graphite (i.e., carbon) and fiberglass are the main options when choosing blank material. Graphite is more expensive than fiberglass, but is lighter and more sensitive. Solid graphite blanks offer more sensitivity than tubular ones.

Properly engineered graphite blanks feature fast, sensitive tips with the strength needed to set hooks and play large fish. A graphite rod with fast action provides the stiffness but also the tip flex needed to let anglers quiver jigs – a presentation to master on ice if you want to entice shy

Longer rods, like the 40-inch pictured here used by Davis Viehbeck, offer plenty of fish-fighting leverage that's needed for icing big predators, like lake trout.

biters. Anglers who want to feel hits should go with graphite because of its superior sensitivity.

In absolute terms, fiberglass blanks are not as sensitive as graphite, but high-end fiberglass gives graphite a run for its money. Fiberglass bends more along the blank than graphite, resulting in smooth hook sets, and premium blanks will stay stiff enough to play big fish. Fiberglass is more resilient than graphite in freezing temperatures, making them a preferred choice for anglers who are not interested in coddling gear. Fiberglass blanks are also preferred for dead-sticking rods because the limber tip signals light hits and lets anglers see the minnow's action. Plus, the blank's forgiving bend gives little resistance during the take.

Although it's wise to consider blank material, there are plenty of quality ice rods on the market. A quality rod will cost a bit more, but it's worth it for the sensitivity and fish-playing features it will deliver.

Other Rod Features

The number and quality of eyes on a rod impact its performance. The more guides, the more uniform the rod bend and the better the blank will absorb shock. Look for short rods with at least four guides and strive for ones with five guides, especially in longer sticks. Eyes will taper in size towards the tip.

Pay attention to the size of a rod's line guides too. Smaller eyes are great for inside a heated shelter or in mild weather as they reduce rod weight, but they can be challenging to use in freezing temperatures. Ice will build up and block small guides, preventing line from easily sliding through. In cold conditions this will quickly hamper your efficiency. Large diameter guides let ice-beaded line pass through more easily than smaller eyes and will reduce the frequency with which you'll need to clean ice off your line and out of the guides. Oversized eyes really pay off if you know you're going to be frequently reeling up and dropping baits in the extreme cold.

Rod handles are also something to keep in mind. Foam and plastic are the least sensitive. They can sometimes absorb water as well, making them uncomfortable to use in freezing temperatures. Cork is preferred by most ice anglers because it conducts vibrations from the blank, repels water, and warms easily when held. Some rod companies also produce high-tech graphite handles.

Handles can have different reel mounting options, from locking

Fiberglass vs Carbon ≫

Fiberglass is phenomenal in situations where you want to watch for bites with a noodle tip rod as an example. It's also extremely durable. Solid carbon, or graphite, blanks are very light and sensitive. These are great for small, micro-maneuver jigging moves where you're barely twitching and bobbing the rod tip while using a pencil grip. A light rod lets you jig like this all day without experiencing fatigue or getting sloppy or bouncy with the rod tip.

Jason Mitchell, Ice Fishing Guide and Rod Designer, ND

Photo: Jason Mitchell

tachment for collecting line. Both set-ups are best used for shallow water conditions for small fish, when hand-landing fish will suffice. Spinning rod combos are only marginally more expensive and have replaced these styles of rods for many anglers.

Storing and Transporting your Rods and Reels

Protecting your rods when not in use keeps them organized and prevents lines from tangling. A rod case also reduces the chances of breaking a stick in transit and shields reels from snow and ice.

There are a variety of rod cases on the market. Some models provide a hard-plastic shell for extra protection. When selecting a rod carrier, keep in mind you'll want enough space to hold at least three rod and reel combos. Durable and large zippers will ensure easy on-ice operation with gloves. Adjustable straps will also help you to shoulder your rods when moving. Lastly, look for cases that have extra storage pockets for tackle trays and other items.

Rod Holders

Also worth considering in terms of rod protection are rod holders designed to secure sticks when fishing. There's plenty of selection in holders and popular options include stand-alone supports that are placed directly on

Many anglers are fond of quality small-sized reels (like this Shimano Symetre) as they balance nicely on an ice rod and feature reliable drag systems.

Cases keep rods protected during travel.

the ice, clip-on models for pails, or holders that you mount in portable or permanent shelters. Although these holders differ in design, the benefits are the same: they keep your rod and reel out of harm's way and off the ice, protected from slush and water that can impede their operation.

TIP-UPS

Tip-ups are stand-alone units that suspend a bait in the water. They feature a signaling device (often a flag) which is tripped when a fish takes the bait. Tip-ups are made mainly from wood or high-impact plastic with some metal parts. The major difference in models is whether the spool sits above or below water, and that's how I'll categorize tip-ups in this overview. Quality models in both categories are designed for easy set-up in the cold and can be compacted for storage during travel.

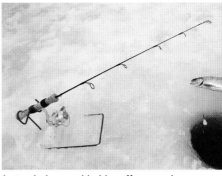

A stand-alone rod holder offers good, simple protection for your rod and reel.

Below-Water Tip-Ups

Below-water tip-ups consist of a frame that lies on the ice and over the hole. The spool shaft is placed in the water, positioned vertically in the hole. One end holds the spool while the other has a trip mechanism. When a fish takes the bait, it's pulling line off the spool which releases the trip mechanism and springs the signaling flag. The positioning of these models over the ice hole and their low profile prevents them from being blown over in strong winds.

Examples of this style of tip-up are the Frabill Arctic Fire Tip-Up, HT Enterprises Polar Tip-Up, Berkley Ice Tip-Up, and Beaver Dam Arctic Fisherman Tip-Up. The spool will not freeze or jam underwater and all models have spool shafts filled with low-temperature lubrication to ensure smooth operation. Some tip-ups also feature a large capacity spool, which is a bonus for targeting big fish like pike or lake trout known to pull plenty of line, or to fish deeper areas. Adjustable spool tension is another feature to look for when chasing big fish under the ice. You need a bit of pressure on the spool to prevent water current or a lively minnow from pulling out line.

A below-water tip-up holds the spool underwater, where it won't freeze.

Some below-water models, including the Frabill Pro-Thermal and HT Enterprises Polar Therm, have circular bases large enough to cover the entire hole and delay freeze-up. The cover also prevents snow from building up in the hole.

Another style of below water tip-ups are built on an "X" frame, like HT Enterprises Mammoth, and have a different trip mechanism consist-

Ken Whiting sets a below-water tip-up.

HT Enterprises' Windlass above-water Tip-Up.

ing of a bent wire shaft that unhooks a signaling flag. Another variation in underwater tip-up design involves magnetic triggered strike indicators, like HT Enterprises Magnetic Polar Pop-Up Tip-Up. The spring-loaded flag rests in the tube body, while the spool sits in the water. The unit itself is supported by fold-out legs that straddle the ice hole. Tension settings can be adjusted to signal even the faintest hits.

Above-Water Tip-Ups

Many above-water spool designs resemble an off-centered "T." In the resting position, a raised arm of the tip-up is balanced over the unit's frame. When a fish hits, the arm lowers, signaling a hit. As a result, these are often called balanced tip-ups. Numerous ice anglers, myself included, experiment with this design and make their own balanced tip-ups.

Another above-water option is HT Enterprises Windlass Tip-Up. A wind-propelled jigging model, this tip-up's rudder catches the breeze and moves the bait up and down, giving you the benefits of a jigging action without needing to move the bait yourself.

The chief disadvantage of above-water tip-ups is exposure to the elements. Moving parts can freeze and potentially malfunction in cold temperatures. They must also be securely anchored so they don't blow over in strong winds or get pulled over by big fish.

A further variation on above-water tip-ups are hybrid models blending tip-up flag strike indicators with rod and reel combos. Some of these models, like the Slamco Slammer Tip-Up and The Automatic Ice Fisherman, are designed to be set by bending and loading the rod, securing the top eye to a trip mechanism. When a fish takes the bait, it trips the unit and the rod unloads, setting the hook on the fish. The Arctic Warrior by Clam Corporation combines the flag strike indicator advantages of a tip-up and a rod holder, letting you fight the fish with a rod (but doesn't automatically set the hook for you like the models noted above).

Tip-up Accessories

There are plenty of accessories on the market to improve the functionality of tip-ups. Lights from companies like HT Enterprises and Frabill can be attached to your tip-up flags and will shine when the flag raises.

Another option are sound-generating strike indicators that alert you when the tip-up is tripped. Strike Sensor makes a transmitter and pager combination, and you can monitor multiple tip-ups from a single device.

A simple but highly effective tool for setting tip-ups are clip-on depth finders. Nothing more than a clip attached to a weight, typically weighing around 1/2- to 3/4-ounces, these gadgets make finding bottom easy when not using electronics. The clip-on weight lets you quickly drop your line to bottom, so there's no guessing the depth. Then remove the clip and retrieve line to factor in where you want your bait positioned near bottom.

ICE FISHING LINE

Quality ice fishing line is an integral part of your angling system. It must be sensitive enough to transmit strikes and be strong enough to hold knots as well as handle the abrasion when a fish occasionally pulls the line across the bottom of your ice hole. Ice line should perform in cold temperatures while still remaining limp enough to easily wind on a spool.

Choosing the best line can be overwhelming. Here's a run-down of the variety of line types on the market, their pros and cons, and what applications they're best suited for. Regardless of which type of line you choose, it's wise to use products branded for ice fishing. You might not notice a difference in mild weather, but when the mercury plummets these brands will deliver.

Nylon-Based Lines

Lines made of nylon have been in the angling industry for decades. You'll see monofilament and copolymer used to described nylon-based fishing line. The advantages of these lines are that they're inexpensive, handle well, and can be used for a variety of fishing applications. They're also available in a range of diameters and breaking strengths, covering off a variety of sport fish species. These lines serve as economical options for jigging rod set-ups and tip-up leads. Berkley Trilene Micro Ice and Cold Weather line, Cortland Ice, Gamma Technologies ESP Ice, HT Enterprises Ice Red, Stren Ice, and Sufix Ice Magic are some examples of these lines.

Fluorocarbon

Fluorocarbon has invaded ice fishing as it has the open water industry. The benefit to fluorocarbon is that its refractive index is similar to water. This makes it almost invisible underwater, a definite benefit when angling shallow, clear water for fussy fish. Fluoro is stiffer than nylon-based lines

Tip-Up Tip »

Use a hair elastic to secure the spool shaft against the frame of underwater tip-ups during transport and storage. They're inexpensive and don't become as brittle as rubber bands do in the cold.

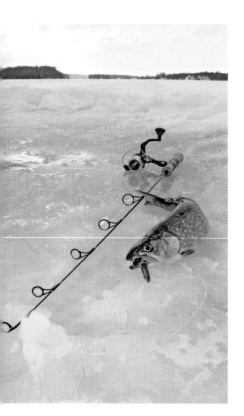

so it transmits vibrations well. It's also extremely resistant to abrasion. All of these traits are beneficial to ice anglers, especially when using small diameter lines. Gamma Technologies FC Ice, Triple Fish Fluorocarbon Ice and Seaguar's Abrazx Ice are 100% fluorocarbon. P-Line Floroice is a copolymer with a fluorocarbon coating. Also worth noting is fluorocarbon is available as a leader material, which is stiffer. Some anglers use these leads at the end of superline for a less visible line connection to the lure and to reduce bite-offs from surprise pike attacks when after other species.

Superlines

Superline is a term used to describe braided and fused lines. The process for making these lines is as their names suggest. Braid is created by weaving several strands of Dyneema or Spectra fibers together. Treated fibers that are fused together are the second category of superlines. Berkley FireLine Micro Ice, Cortland Braided Ice, PowerPro Ice, Rapala Ice Braid Titanium, Stren Microfuse Ice, and Sufix Performance Ice Braid are popular superlines. Both processes result in a single strand of tough, thin-diameter line with excellent strength and minimal stretch. These traits give anglers an incredible feel and excellent hook-setting power. To give some context to the advantages of the thin diameter, a superline may deliver the breaking strength of 8-pound test at a diameter akin to traditional 2-pound test monofilament.

Most ice superlines are treated with a coating to prevent water retention, an inherent weakness of untreated fibers. Although it's more expensive than monofilament, one spool of superline can often last you several seasons. A word of caution though: Stick to using superlines for jigging and rod applications and don't use them on tip-ups. Superline can slice through fingers if you're hand-fighting a fish.

Another superline option is tying on a monofilament or fluorocarbon leader of a few feet. Join the lines with a small swivel or back to back uni knots. This set up delivers superline's no-stretch advantage with the low visibility properties of the added leader.

Nylon and Dacron Tip-up Line

The last category of line I want to touch on is 20- to 40-pound test nylon or dacron for tip-ups. Both types deliver excellent strength and abrasion resistance. Their thick diameter also makes them easier for hand-fighting

Ice anglers have plenty of line options to choose from. The top two rows are a sampling of superline, fluorocarbon, copolymer and monofilament options. The bottom row (left) are common tip-up lines, while the three spools to the right are examples of sevenstrand wire and fluorocarbon leader material.

Photo: Dave Genz

fish. Often lines are sold in black, red, or green so they're easy to spot on the ice. To prevent lines from spooking fish, attach a leader of monofilament, copolymer, fluorocarbon line, or wire. A spooled tip-up can last for several seasons, making nylon or dacron economical over the long run. You can also purchase vinyl or PVC coated lines to stop water absorption and prevent freezing. Berkley, Cortland, Frabill, and HT Enterprises are just a few companies making tip-up lines.

LURES, BAITS, AND TERMINAL TACKLE

Tackle gets a lot of air time from anglers. When someone is getting into consistent fishing action, we want to know what lure type, color, and size they're using. Of course the questions of what type of area were you fishing and how you were working the bait are perhaps even more important, but those are details (along with specific lures) I'll get into in the fish-specific chapters of Part II of this book. In this section, I want to lay the groundwork by reviewing the common types of tackle associated with ice fishing.

Jigging Spoons

Jigging spoons are among the most popular lures because they're well matched for the vertical presentation inherent in sitting over an ice hole. When worked properly, spoons will attract and intrigue fish enough to bite. Their slender profile mimics a minnow and they come in a plethora of sizes and color patterns. Another common feature in spoons is the addition of rattle chambers to boost vibrations that attract fish. Their shape varies too: wide-bodied and bent spoons glide and flutter to the sides more than thinner or straight-profiled ones, which drop faster with a more reserved action. At times, each has their place on the ice, so carrying an assortment of different shapes and sizes will ensure you're properly outfitted.

Jigging Minnows

Jigging minnows, also called swimming lures, have a horizontal, minnow-like profile. On slack line, their small rear fins cause the bait to glide and lets anglers work a wider area of water under the ice hole. In the hands of an expert, jigging minnows come alive and can fool even the most reluctant biters. These baits come in a range of sizes from roughly 1- to

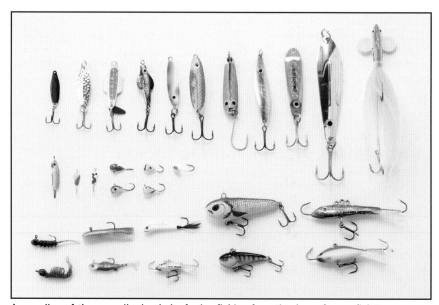

A sampling of the many jigging baits for ice fishing from tiny lures for panfish to big-profiled offerings for walleye, pike, and lake trout.

3.5-inches in length. For the sake of this brief overview, rattle, blade and darter baits can also be loosely lumped into this horizontal lure category.

Ice Jigs

In the simplest definition, jigs are hooks with a weight molded on them. Variations in the jig's shape, size, hook orientation, and paint pattern are what makes this category of tackle so vast. There are micro baits designed to mimic aquatic invertebrates, vertical and horizontal models, tear drops, and winged jigs designed to glide as they drop.

Northland's Puppet Minnow.

Plastics and Soft Baits

Plastics and soft baits are often used to add profile and action to plain jigs. Some are infused with scent to tempt inquisitive fish into biting. Twister tail grubs, hollow tubes, and thin, tapered tails are some popular types of plastic baits available. Artificial maggots, freshwater shrimp, nymphs, and crayfish are some other common creature shapes found in soft baits.

Lure Nuances: Color, Glow, Prism Tape, and Rattles

It's worth taking a moment to touch on some different lure details. Anglers vary in how much stock they place in the notion that color has fish-catching effects. Overall, I think that getting particular about color should come well after you've located fish, have found a jigging sequence they're interested in, and are concerned with refining your strategy.

What I also know, however, is that certain hues and paint patterns can and do make a big difference. During low-light or dark conditions, glow baits have dramatically improved my hook-up rates for walleye and crappie. For this reason, I always carry several spoons, jigging minnows, and ice jigs with glow paint patterns. Also pack a small LED flashlight as you need to regularly shine the light on the bait for it to glow. Once the glow fades, charge it again with another few seconds of light.

I also think color can be pivotal during midwinter conditions, cold fronts, heavy pressured community holes, and other factors that contribute to tough bites. If you look in the tackle trays of serious anglers, you'll see they have a rainbow of bait colors. Two-toned baits can help narrow down what colors are hot on a given day. Get your fishing buddies to try different patterns and you can isolate popular hues even faster. Be sure to carry a mix of colors including whites, chartreuses, pinks, oranges, various glow hues, browns, blacks, and beiges.

Berkley Gulp! makes a great tipping bait to boost scent, color, and profile of lures.

Brendan Mark lands a 13.5-inch crappie taken on a glow, finesse plastic by Northland.

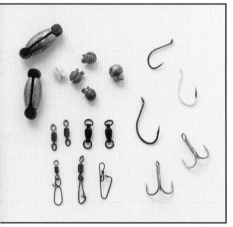

An ice angler's tackle box should carry an assortment of terminal tackle, including various sinkers, single and treble hooks, swivels, snap-swivels, and snaps.

Glittering metal also attracts its fair share of bites, and indeed, gold- or silver-plated spoons are sometimes even more effective than painted lures because of the high degree of flash they emit when jigging. One example that comes to mind was during an outing with friend, Derek Samson. We were targeting lake trout on a 50-foot, mid-lake hump. We had several fish zoom in to inspect our spoons, but we couldn't trigger bites. The strategy was simple: cycle through different profiles and colors of baits until we cracked the code. It didn't take long. Turns out they wanted a silver offering that, we later discovered when cleaning a few small fish we kept for a meal, matched their forage perfectly. Once we both switched to silver we iced quite a few of these cold-water scrappers. Of course, savvy bait companies have found ways to offer anglers the best of both worlds by selling spoons with a metallic sheen on one side and paint or prism tape on the other. You can also purchase different patterns and colors of prism tape to add your own custom touch to favorite lures.

In addition to visuals, sound can also sometimes increase your catch. Rattle baits are worth carrying in your tackle box to help attract fish with jigging sequences. Shaking a bait to send a clatter out through the water has worked for me with several species, including walleye, pike and lake trout, as well as inquisitive perch and crappie.

Terminal Tackle

Beyond lures and baits, there are some other pieces of terminal tackle you should carry. Here's a quick list.

Snaps and Swivels

Snaps let you clip on baits without needing to cut and re-tie every time you change lures. They're particularly handy when working large spoons and jigging minnows but aren't intended to be used with a smaller, finesse presentation. Swivels prevent line twist. They can also be used to join main lines and leaders together. Use ball bearing swivels for the best performance. A snap-swivel combines both of these components into one piece of hardware.

Hooks

You'll want to carry an assortment of hooks on the ice if fishing with bait. I'll discuss specific sizes and types of hooks in the species sections. Octopus, treble, circle, and bait hooks are commonly used in ice fishing.

Weights and Sinkers

Weights help get your bait to a desired depth and keep it in this area. Often this is near bottom, but not always. As a general rule, use just enough weight to anchor a bait; over-weighting a line increases the chance a fish will feel resistance when it bites and drop the lure before you can set the hook. You'll need more weight in deep water, areas with heavy current, or when using large or lively minnows. Weights are often used with tip-ups or when dead-sticking bait. Split shot and rubber core sinkers are common ice fishing weights. Their design allows for adjustable positioning on the line and they can be taken off and re-used.

Leaders and Wire

When targeting toothy predators like pike, using a leader is critical to preventing bite-offs and landing fish. Stranded wire is the most common for ice fishing. Many pre-rigged leaders are available and you can also make your own by purchasing components and wire, such as Berkley Sevenstrand uncoated wire in 27-pound test. Titanium provides another effective leader material for toothy critters. Wire continues to be the mainstay for toothy fish or when in dingy water, but fluorocarbon leader material is also gaining popularity (as noted above) in the 40- to 60-pound test range.

Floats

Floats are another tool anglers can use to help detect strikes. Slip floats let you adjust a stopper on your line and where your bait is presented in the water column. Clip-on models are effective as well. Weighted floats might seem like an oxymoron, but these models are closer to being neutrally buoyant so they move at even the lightest strike. Floats perform best in sheltered conditions from wind and where ice-hole freeze-up can be delayed.

Keeping it Organized: Tackle Trays

With an abundance of different tackle to choose from on the ice, tackle trays and storage boxes are essential for keeping it tidy. Organizing your tackle makes you more efficient on the ice because you'll know exactly where you've stored specific lures. Protecting that tackle will also prolong its lifespan.

Keep 'em Sharp »

Having spare hooks is important to replace damaged or inferior ones on lures. Swapping out the weak and the dull with sharp and the strong is an easy way to boost the number of fish you catch. This Buck-Shot Spoon has seen a fair share of fish and bottom contact so a Gamakatsu treble hook is used to replace the original.

Simple Storage »

Old film canisters are great for storing small items like jigs, hooks, or sinkers.

Gord Ellis, Outdoor Journalist & Professional Angler, ON

Invest in trays with quality latches and regularly inspect the condition of the snaps for wear. Most ice anglers I know opt for tackle trays of varying sizes to organize their tackle. Clear plastic cases make finding the right bait easy.

Small, low-profile boxes like those used by fly anglers are great for carrying ice jigs and small baits. Their compact size lets you stuff them in jacket and pant pockets without feeling their bulk.

LIVE BAIT AND CONTAINERS

Using live bait alone or to tip lures is common practice on the ice. Minnows, maggots, and waxworms are the most popular bait options. To store minnows for extended periods in cold weather, keep them in an insulated minnow bucket. Frabill and Plano make buckets with insulated liners that delay the water from freezing in sub-zero temperatures. Another useful accessory to use to outfit minnow pails is a battery-powered aerator to pump a continuous supply of oxygen in the water. This is

The Rose Creek Anglers Polar Box makes an excellent container for carrying and organizing ice jigs.

The pocket-sized Bait Puck by StrikeMaster is perfect for carrying maggots to be used for tipping baits.

particularly handy to keep minnows lively overnight during multi-day adventures. Finally, opt for a minnow dip net with a floating handle. It's best to fish out minnows with the net rather than dipping your hand in cold water. I'm as guilty as the next person for forgetting or misplacing a net – so I've learned to carry a spare – but you can sometimes get by with an ice skimmer too.

You always know a community is serious about ice fishing (especially for panfish) when their tackle shops stock fresh maggots and waxworms. You can pack a surprisingly large number of these grubs in a small container. Two options are the Strike Master Bait Pucks and Lindy Grub Getter. In extreme cold, keep the container inside a jacket to prevent the bait from freezing. Adding a bit of fresh sawdust or wood shavings will help keep the critters' environment comfy, but don't use cuttings from treated wood as these will likely kill your bait.

FISHING TOOLS

There are several types of tools worth carrying on the ice. The first category is catch and release items. A pair of long-nosed pliers is useful for removing hooks and avoiding a fish's sharp teeth. Fishing-specific models sometimes come with excellent grips and leaf springs that make them easier to operate with a pair of gloves on in cold temperatures. If you're targeting small-mouthed fish or using smaller hooks, a pair of forceps or hemostats are better than bulky pliers.

Carry a quality pair of scissors or clippers for cutting line. Another item you'll want to have within reach is a file for touching up hooks. Keeping points ultra-sharp increases the odds of a quality hook set, and also makes live bait tipping easier.

Two other important tools straddle the categories of fishing and safety. These are boot cleats for additional traction on bare, slippery ice conditions and ice picks to help you pull yourself out of the water should you fall through ice. I provide more details on these items in Chapter 6.

OTHER USEFUL GEAR

In addition to the staple ice fishing stuff, here are some of my other tried-and-true items that are sure to keep you properly outfitted on your outings.

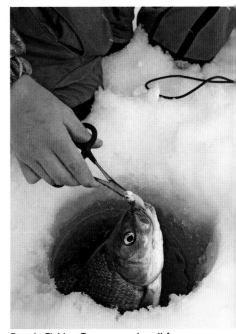

Rapala Fishing Forceps work well for removing baits on small to medium-sized fish, like this whitefish. Their coated handle makes them more comfortable to use in winter with bare hands than all-metal versions.

On-Ice Illumination: Headlamps, Lanterns, and Lights

Consider carrying a portable light when ice fishing. Even if you don't intend to set up, fish, or leave in the dark, a hot bite can often extend the duration of an outing.

I've found the most useful light is a headlamp. The hands-free operation makes it easy to illuminate whatever I need. I like small, compact LED headlamps. I pack one with my gear and take it on every outing, so that I'm ready to go for those unexpected night fishes. An alternative to these small compact models are the clip-on hat lights.

Battery or fuel powered lanterns make up the next category of lights you'll often see ice anglers using. The benefit to using propane or gas models is that in addition to putting out plenty of light, they also generate heat to keep you warm on dark, cold outings. These lanterns are bulkier than headlamps, but can be worth it if you've got the space. Crappie and walleye anglers often use these units when fishing on time-proven spots to try their nighttime luck for these low light feeders.

Beyond headlamps and lanterns, there are plenty of other lights you can use on the ice. Small LED lights can be perfect for charging up glow-painted lures. Traditional flashlights can also serve as back-up. There are also shelter lighting options, from clip-on portable lights to permanent mount lights.

Heaters

Many ice anglers rely on the warmth of portable heaters to keep them comfortable when fishing. Propane heaters are excellent choices for heating portable and permanent ice huts. Look for models with adjustable heat output settings: sometimes you'll only need the heater on low to keep holes from freezing and keep your hands warm, while on other days you'll want all the heat the unit can produce. Inspect the heat output ratings when buying a heater. One unit I use puts out 4,000 BTUs/Hr on a low setting and 9,000 BTUs/Hr on high, which is a blessing in frigid temperatures when the wind's howling.

Exercise extreme caution when using a heater. Although hundreds of ice anglers use portable, propane heaters to warm their huts, there is a risk associated with using these units in enclosed spaces. Always ensure the heater is secure and stable, to prevent tipping. Beyond the risk of accidental fire, heaters use oxygen and release carbon monoxide during operation. Carbon monoxide is lethal and particularly insidious because

>> **Battery Power**

Cold weather can wreak havoc on battery life, so carry spare batteries and keep them warm by storing them inside your jacket to prevent the cold from draining them.

it's odorless, so it's also essential to have an open vent providing fresh air (check the heater's manual for recommended vent size). If when using a heater inside a fish house you experience a headache, dizziness and/or nausea these are signs of carbon monoxide poisoning - seek fresh air immediately! Some heaters, like Mr. Heater's Buddy Heaters, come with an automatic low-oxygen detector that turns the unit off if oxygen falls below a safe level. Portable heaters can keep you toasty on the ice and help return dexterity and comfort to cold hands, but always take extreme care when using them.

It's a good practice to carry a shovel on your ice fishing adventures. Use it to clear snow from drilled holes, seal in the tent fabric on a portable shelter, or dig your vehicle out of a snow drift if you get stuck (it happens). Rapala's Folding Pack Shovel is a great, compact option.

A snow machine, power auger, portable sonar, and a quality rod and reel combo are just a sampling of equipment pro ice anglers, like Dave Bennett, use to catch fish through the ice.

Backpacks

This last item joins me on every ice outing I take. Backpacks are extremely handy for carrying the day's water and food, packing extra clothing layers, and storing a variety of other items. As you'll likely load your backpack up with gear, I'd recommend getting one with a waist belt. The belt will transfer the pack's weight from your shoulders to your hips for a more comfortable fit. Another useful feature in packs is side-long zippers. Unlike top loading models, these backpacks let you access items in the pack no matter where they're located. This is helpful when fumbling with gloves or mitts in cold temperatures.

Wrap Up

There's no denying the abundance of ice fishing gear available. If you're new to the hard-water game, don't be intimidated by all of this equipment. The reality is that one or two rod and reel combos spooled with quality ice line and an assortment of lures are all you need to get started. That is, all you need in addition to one more crucial item: an auger or spud to break through the ice. Aside from these items, everything else falls into the categories of keeping you more comfortable or helping you specialize your fishing strategies.

ICE BREAKERS

ICE BREAKERS

Wherever you're fishing, whatever you're fishing, every hard-water angler faces the same initial hurdle: you can't fish until you make a hole in the ice. Cutting and chipping through ice is part of the game when it comes to winter angling. Things will go smoothly provided you've got the right tools to do the job. The main way to get through the ice is by using a hand or power auger, and there's plenty of choice for both types. Hole diameter, handles, weight, and blade types are a sampling of what you'll want to consider when choosing an auger.

In this chapter, I'll look at these items in detail as well as other ice-burrowing accessories such as chippers and skimmers, along with tips on how to use them. Keeping these techniques in mind will make cutting ice holes easier and faster, and a fine-honed technique will be gentler on your equipment.

MANUAL AUGERS

Manual augers are completely powered by human strength. Turning the handle causes the auger to spin and the blades to cut. Anglers admire these augers for their simplicity and ease of operation. The catch is that you need to have enough energy to crank the handle, and after drilling several holes through thick ice, your vigor might well begin to wane.

Lightweight and compact, hand augers are easy to transport, which accounts for much of their appeal. Hand augers often range between 5- and 10-pounds, and are significantly lighter than power models, which are typically between 25- and 35-pounds. This is a big bonus for anglers carrying their own gear and makes manual augers particularly suitable for long on-ice hikes and backcountry exploring. Many models feature collapsible handles for easy storage and transportation. Others have adjustable handle lengths, letting you customize the auger to match your height or to suit the thickness of the ice you're cutting. And as you'd expect, another advantage of hand augers is cost: they're relatively inexpensive and a fraction of the price of power models.

StrikeMaster's Strike-Lite, 4-Stroke power auger makes quick work of cutting holes.

There are some features to consider if you're buying a hand auger. One is the type of blades. Curved blades, found in models such as the StrikeMaster Lazer Hand Auger and Normark Fin-Bore III, are designed to cut ice more aggressively with less effort than the flat blades found on traditional augers.

Offset handles are another feature to look for in hand augers. This handle design delivers more torque, making drilling less taxing and more efficient. If you're used to drilling with a conventional hand auger, it will take you a short while to get the feel for the mechanics of an offset grip, but the adjustment is worth it. The Normark Fin-Bore III is an example of an auger with this feature.

The diameter of the ice hole should be matched to the size of the species you're after. Four-inch holes can be good for perch, while 5-inch ones work for most panfish. Six-inch holes can accommodate other species like walleye and whitefish. An 8-inch hole or bigger is best for larger species. When choosing a hole diameter to cut with your hand auger, keep in mind that the larger the hole, the more energy it will take to cut through the ice.

POWER AUGERS

When faced with thick ice, it's tough to beat a power auger. These units drill holes fast and allow you to make plenty of them quickly. You can be fishing within minutes with minimal fatigue, whereas cutting several holes in thick ice with a hand auger can be strenuous. For extremely thick

Light and compact, manual augers are the perfect tool for walk-in lakes.

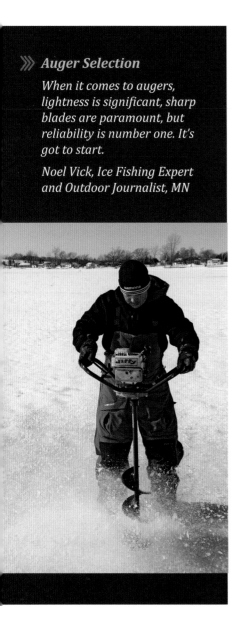

ice, companies sell extensions to increase drill length. And not only do power augers make quick work of even the thickest ice, they're also better than hand augers for drilling larger holes. StrikeMaster, Jiffy Ice Drills, Eskimo, Normark, and Nils Master all make power augers.

These augers are powered with gas or electrical engines. Some are even designed to be operated with a cordless drill. As with any power tool, regular maintenance is essential for proper performance. You'll also need to transport gas or batteries for your power auger. Mixing gas and oil is standard practice on most augers that have two-stroke motors, although StrikeMaster's Strike-Lite is a 4-stroke auger that eliminates this mixing chore. This auger is extremely light for a power model (20lbs).

The trade-off of power augers is their weight and bulk. This likely isn't an issue if you're towing your gear on the ice with a snow machine or ATV, but if you're on foot and pulling a sled, it's worth considering. You must contemplate the pros and cons between weighing down your sled and the tool's ice-cutting ability.

Power augers cost considerably more than manual ones. If you're an intermediate or hard-core ice angler, you likely own a power auger, or you're debating buying one. For beginners or those who don't fish very often during winter, the cost can be delayed until you become more serious about ice fishing or your lifestyle allows more outings.

Maintaining Your Auger

Your auger is absolutely critical to ice fishing. If it fails, you're packing up and going home, unless you brought a spare manual auger as a back up, which is good practice. Here are some maintenance tips to keep your auger in top shape for plenty of winter adventures.

Keep the blades sharp. This begins by always having them covered when not in use. It's also critical not to bang the blades on the ice. This can dull or nick them. After drilling holes, shake off or let water drip off the drill, and return the cover to the auger's blades.

After each outing, carefully dry blades with a towel and then spray a water-displacing lubricant on them to prevent rusting. Corrosion dulls blades and makes cutting more difficult. Some companies sell blade sharpeners for touching up edges. Once blades get overly worn or nicked, though, you'll need to replace them altogether with new ones; how frequently you'll need to do this will depend on how often you fish and how well you take care of them.

Before every outing, check the tightness of the blades and the shaft connection. Vibrations and usage can loosen these bonds. If you're using a power auger, ensure gas and oil levels are topped up as well. Also consider assembling and carrying an auger tool supply kit. It should contain a wrench to change and tighten blades, an extra set of blades, a spare strap for the blade cover, and a replacement spark plug for power models.

Manual augers require minimal care during the off-season: simply coat the blades with oil and store them in a dry place. For power augers, read your owner's manual. You'll need to prepare your auger's engine for long-term storage; the off-season is also the time to get it serviced. Contact the engine company for a listing of certified repair shops in your area. Your manual will also give you a maintenance schedule for other parts, such as air filters. Once your engine has been serviced and you've done any other maintenance work, cover the power head to keep debris from collecting on the engine. At the start of the season, test the engine before the first outing. At a minimum, clean or replace the spark plug.

Drilling Holes

Now that we've covered the two main types of augers, I want to share some tips for using them to drill holes. Over the years, I've seen a variety of different techniques for starting, drilling, and removing slush and ice

Sharp auger blades are a must for fast, efficient cutting.

Your Auger at Rest

Although it looks neat in photos, storing an auger in a half-drilled hole on the ice isn't recommended. On mild days you can likely get away with it, but in freezing temperatures you risk the auger freezing into the ice. Removing it can result in damage to the drill and engine on power models. It's best to lay the auger down on the ice in an area cleared of snow. Putting a wet auger in deep snow in freezing temperatures can cause problems. The snow will quickly turn to slush on the drill and then freeze, coating the blades with ice which can impact performance. The manual for your power model should recommend which end of the engine should face up.

shards from holes. Whether you're using a manual or power auger will in part determine the best method. Here are some things to keep in mind the next time you put blades to ice.

The first thing to do is to choose your location wisely. Whenever possible, drill over snow as opposed to bare ice for the extra traction the snow affords. Also, sometimes fish will hide under shadows created by patches of snow, so you might find fishing better in snow-covered areas. Also drill over clean ice. Avoid spots where vehicles park as deposits of sand and salt from road slush can dull and damage blades. It's common in permanent ice shacks to re-open frozen holes. In this case, an auger with a chipper-style blade is best. Doing it with other auger blade types will dull them faster than drilling through fresh ice. The other option to open up old holes is using a chisel, a tool I'll cover momentarily.

Before drilling, tuck in loose clothing or items (like a lanyard) that may catch and tangle in the auger engine. Next, stabilize your footing and take a wide stance. This helps you control the auger better. Whether you're using a power or manual auger, let the blades do the cutting. What I mean by this is that you don't need to apply a lot of downward pressure on the auger. Often, the weight of the power auger itself is sufficient. With manuals, more pressure is needed to start the hole, but once you've bored a groove you can back off on the pressure. Pushing hard won't make the auger cut faster. In fact, it could even slow you down, because you'll tire out more quickly. Over time you'll learn the exact amount of pressure you need to start and drill holes so you can save your energy. As you approach the bottom end of the ice, you'll likely notice more resistance. Continue cutting and keep a firm grip on the auger as you break through the frozen barrier.

Once you bore through the ice, there are several ways to remove the auger and clear out most of the slush. If you're using a manual auger, try these steps: After cutting through the ice, water will begin to rise up in the hole. Before it reaches the top, kick away the ice mound with your boots. When finished, stand further back from the hole than when you were drilling. By this time, the water will have likely risen to the top of the hole and you'll be ready to remove the auger and slush. With the auger's blades at the bottom of the hole, use a quick upward motion and pull it straight up out of the hole. This will remove a lot of the slush and ice, letting it fall to the sides and clearing out most of the hole.

With power augers, you can often use the spinning drill to carry ice up and out of the hole. One trick shared with me by Dave Genz is to kick

A quick lift with a manual auger is a good tactic to clear out most slush and ice shards.

away only a portion of the ice mound. This cleared area will channel out slush, so make sure your feet aren't in front of it or they risk getting wet. Simply run the auger briefly until most of the slush rises and flows out of the slush-mound opening. Remember to avoid kicking wet slush with your boots to reduce the chances of getting your feet wet.

Chisels

Chisels (sometimes called spuds) are tools used to help break through the ice. Chisels consist of a sharp blade at the end of a long, heavy bar. Using downward jabs, anglers use these tools to reopen holes in permanent shelters or to break through thin ice.

Chisels tend to be less expensive than hand augers but have limitations. Beyond clearing holes in shelters, they're best reserved for thin-ice conditions. They also make a fair amount of noise when you're punching through the ice, discounting them as an option for stealth angling for skittish fish. Still, chisels have their place and when used as intended, they're an effective tool.

Some anglers use chisels as a walking stick or ice thickness tester, punching the spud ahead of them as they tread slowly on the ice. If the spud breaks through on one attempt the ice is too thin: it's unsafe and should be vacated immediately. Ice safety is a vitally important subject, and I cover it in more detail in Chapter 6.

Skimmers

A skimmer, also called a scoop, is an inexpensive piece of equipment you don't want to forget on your outings. It looks like an oversized ladle with holes and is designed to scoop out the ice to clear fishing holes. Not only is this common practice to remove remaining ice from newly-drilled holes, but in freezing temperatures you'll need to skim out a layer of ice whether you're jigging or using tip-ups.

Plastic skimmers are light, but become brittle when cold. Metal skimmers are heavier but take more abuse. Some have rulers on their handles for measuring your catch, while others come with small chippers at the end. Handles come in a variety of lengths as well. The Ice Scoop by Frabill lets you clean out holes without bending over and the large-sized scoop makes quick work of removing slush.

Drilling in Tandem ≫

I often abandon power augers in shallow, clear water situations, or any time I'm fishing for stream trout. I prefer the stealth of a hand auger. However, it is still extremely important to drill a lot of holes and stay mobile. To keep from getting worn out when using a hand auger use a two-man technique. Have two anglers grab the auger handle in the same spots, the second man's hands over the top of the first person's hands. Do not stand directly across from each-other. Both of you will reach the weakest points of the drilling motion at the same time. Instead stand at an angle. Then simply drill the holes together.

Jacob Edson, Editor Ice Fishing magazine, WI

Be sure to carry a skimmer to clean slush from ice holes. Pictured here is Rapala's Ice Scoop.

Wrap Up

Tunneling through the ice to access winter's frigid waters is part of the ice fishing game. The good news is that because augers and chisels are mandatory items for all anglers, there are plenty of options for any budget and style of fishing. Like most anglers I know, I started out with a manual auger, and graduated to a power model once my angling became more serious and the cost justifiable. Throughout the season, I use both manual and power augers depending on my target species, when I'm fishing, and how far I plan to lug my equipment around.

I once had a friend – a non-angler – tease me by saying fishing is as much about the gear as it is about catching fish. This was obviously in jest, but he raised a valid point: there's a lot of stuff associated with any type of angling and ice fishing is no exception. The difference between a "need" and a "want" varies from one angler to another. If you're just trying ice fishing and can borrow an auger from a friend, that's handy, but otherwise an auger clearly belongs on the "needs" list once you decide to start ice fishing on a regular basis. In the next chapter I'll be talking about shelters. A quality portable shelter is an interesting case when it comes to distinguishing between ice fishing wants and needs. Fishing without one isn't a major issue on calm, mild winter days, but once you've used one in cold and windy conditions, odds are you'll wonder how you ever angled effectively without a shelter.

SHELTERS

SHELTERS

Shelters are central to ice fishing. They block wind, shield you from snow, and can be heated to boost your comfort. The major distinction between shelters is whether they're portable or permanent huts. In ice angling discussions, a "permanent hut" is an ice house that's put on the ice and removed after each season, requiring vehicles and a bit of effort to move them around. You can pull permanent huts across the ice to tweak their positioning, but large moves on the same lake or to different waters is a big undertaking compared to portable shelters. Because of this, I'll mainly be focusing on portable ones in this chapter.

Portable ice huts are a staple of ice fishing. If you're willing to move and drill plenty of holes to find fish, a portable hut is a great supporting tool for a mobility-based approach to ice fishing. In permanent huts, you're forced to wait for the fish to come to you and swim into your trap of fishing lines. Portables however, let you move and locate fish, which is similar to the run-and-gun search methods of open water angling, trying several spots until you find biting fish. In this sense, a portable shelter is your boat on the ice.

There are a variety of portable shelters on the market offering choices in terms of price, size, convenience, and degree of weather protection. In this chapter, I'll give an overview of your options in portable shelters and I'll share advice on what to look for when choosing the best one to suit your needs.

PORTABLE SHELTERS

Windbreaks

Fairly inexpensive, windbreaks are the most basic kind of portable shelter. They have a seat and two or three walls for wind protection. Windbreaks are lightweight, making them an option for hiking to remote lakes. For example, the HT Enterprises Polar Windbreak Ice Fishing Shelter weighs

>> **Windy Wishes**

A lot of anglers know wind can be good for open-water fishing, but it can mean hot action on the ice too. Some of the best times I've been fishing it's been windy. We had to anchor down our shacks and it wasn't fun to drill holes - but it was worth it because the fish were rocking! If you've got the right tools, like a shelter and a heater, and can tolerate the wind, you'll get rewarded.

Steve Barnett, Hard-Core Ice Angler, ON

less than 12-pounds. Unfortunately, windbreaks don't provide overhead protection, leaving you exposed to snow, sleet, and rain. They also don't trap in heat the way a closed shelter does.

Several years ago while fishing a bay on Lake Ontario with friend, Steve Barnett, we observed an angler fishing from a windbreak. Every time he'd move he'd prop up a walking stick for a minute or so, before setting up his shelter. Initially we couldn't figure out what he was doing. Then we realized his strategy. On the top of the stick he had tied a thin piece of cloth that would blow in the breeze revealing its direction. He'd then place his shelter accordingly for the best wind protection.

Collapsible Shelters

Sometimes called pop-ups, these shelters set up quickly and provide full protection from the elements for one or more anglers. Their design resembles a camping tent but is customized for ice fishing. The Eskimo QuickFish 2 and the Frabill Outpost Hub Shelter are two examples of these types of shelters.

Some of these shelters don't have floors and the entire ice surface remains exposed inside their wind-protecting walls. Other models have floors which are made of a lightweight, flexible fabric, unlike the hard-plastic sled of flip-over or cabin-style shelters. These bases have openings to allow for easy fishing. High-end models feature windows and long skirts to prevent drafts. The downside of these shelters is that you need to remove gear and take them down when moving a considerable distance. Short moves can be done with two anglers grabbing the poles and lifting the shelter as they walk to the new location. Similar to tents, some of these shelters can be challenging to set up and anchor in heavy winds. The bonus is that some models can break down to a compact size for storage and transportation in a carrying case. High-end collapsible shelters make good options on trips with weight and size restrictions.

Flip-Over Shelters

Flip-over shelters are extremely popular. Scan a community ice fishing area and you'll see plenty of them. Clam Corporation, Eskimo, Frabill, HT Enterprises, Otter Outdoors, and Shappell Corporation all make flip-over shelters in an array of sizes.

Flip-over models are built on a sled base. The foundation acts as a container to hold belongings during travel and while fishing. This is a big

advantage of these units: rods, electronics, tackle, and other items can be stored in the hut and moved from one spot to the next with ease. The sled base also holds the fishing seats; some are removable, while others are secured on sliding tracks. Many companies sell sled covers. These are worth buying. They keep snow out of your sled and secure its contents during transit, so you don't have to worry about things falling out as you move around.

The sled's sides hold adjustable poles which are the skeleton for the tent canvas. In some respects, the poles operate like the roof of a convertible car, but aren't powered. When you're ready to fish, sit down on the sled chair, extend the poles (if necessary), and flip them over. Suddenly, you're fishing in a canvas tent with a large patch of ice in front of you. Most models have three tent positions: completely open, up halfway for a windbreak, or fully closed. During travel, the poles are lowered with the canvas collected and rested on the top of the sled's sides.

In addition to providing storage in their sleds, the speed with which these shelters can be set up or collapsed for travel is a big reason why they're so popular with ice anglers. They can also be easily attached to snow machines or ATVs using tow bars. Some companies sell accessories such as runners for sled bases to reduce wear and improve towing.

Serge Bricault enjoys the wind-break feature of a flip-over shelter while still soaking up the sun.

Tents also provide protection from wind, rain, and snow. Most flip-over shelters have wide skirts to help cut down on drafts and can be buried in snow for the ultimate in heat retention and wind protection. The tent canvas also blocks out light for sight fishing. If you plan to use a heater, buy a shelter with ventilation options or mesh windows for air flow.

Due to the deep plastic sled, flip-over shelters are heavier than windbreaks or collapsible shelters. The trade-off, however, is well worth it for anglers looking for both wind and snow protection and a sled to carry gear when on the move.

Cabin-Style Shelters

For a more spacious portable ice hut, consider cabin-style shelters. Cabin-style shelters are designed to be roomier than other portable shelters, and are somewhat like permanent ice fishing houses. These models are built on hard-bottom plastic sleds that fold in half for transport. For this reason, they're sometimes called suitcase-style shelters. Cabins come in a range of sizes, and the larger ones comfortably fit several anglers. Clam Corporation, Frabill, HT Enterprises, and Shappell Corporation produce models.

The Frabill Refuge Cabin Style Shelter.

To set up a cabin-style shelter, unfold the floor and extend the poles to pop up the sides and roof of the tent. Most models are high enough to stand in; only a small percentage of flip-over shelters have this much overhead space. The full-sized floor also keeps your feet elevated and up off the ice, helping them to stay warm.

On small models, you can leave the shelter set up to make short moves. These shelters don't offer the deep sleds that flip-over models do, and aren't as effective at transporting gear. For the larger and heavier models, you'll likely need to take them down and fold the sled. Although moving a cabin-style shelter is not an arduous task, it does take more time than moving a flip-over shelter.

Large cabins let you comfortably fish with several anglers, with room for everyone's gear inside. These shelters are a great choice when your trips are more about enjoying company with friends and family and less about making a lot of moves to find fish.

Shelter Features

Here are some features to look for and things to bear in mind when buying a portable hut. Invest in a good-quality model. Inferior equipment won't hold up in cold conditions. Paying extra will also likely land you a more cozy seat – a cushioned chair with a backrest is well worth the money and will keep you comfortable on long outings.

Collapsible and cabin-style shelters come with zipper doors, but they're not standard on all flip-over models. Zipper doors let you exit your shelter without flipping it over. This is handy when you've buried the tent skirt in snow to block out wind and hold in heat. Open the door's zipper slightly and you have another venting option.

Make sure the shelter you buy has windows or a vent on every side. You'll appreciate the light they let in and windows also let you monitor things outside such as tip-ups. Look for windows with a roll-up cover, though, so you can block out light when you want to sight fish.

Tent walls with hanging, mesh compartments are handy for storing items. Some shelters come with small organizers, letting you keep items such as tackle trays, artificial bait containers, and drinks organized but within reach.

Flip-over shelters are built on a sled base, which is great for carrying gear if you'll be moving around.

Before buying a shelter, check the dimensions to ensure it fits in your car. Truck and SUV owners aren't likely to have problems getting shelters into their vehicles, but compact car owners may face some challenges with larger models. You may be able to lower the seats and accommodate the length of a two-person flip-over shelter, but the depth of a large sled may restrict you from sliding it into a small trunk.

In addition to checking out the dimensions, note its weight. There is a wide range within each of the four categories of portable shelters. Some are designed to fit multiple people but can be quite heavy. Be realistic about the amount of weight you can lift on your own and remember that the heavier the sled, the tougher it will be to pull it through deep or wet snow.

PERMANENT ICE HUTS, OR FISH HOUSES

Portables shelters are popular right now, but I do want to touch on permanent shelters (also called fish houses) for a few reasons. For decades, permanent do-it-yourself ice huts were the mainstay of ice fishing outings. Many permanent huts are built by their owners and some design plans are available on-line. Part of the fun of fishing from permanent huts is admiring the builder's engineering ingenuity. Each shelter has a different character and atmosphere to it. The more mobile models will be built on a trailer frame with wheels, making for easy towing with a vehicle to and on the lake. Alternatively, some companies make these houses in a range of styles and sizes from bare-bones basics to models bordering on outdoor luxury. Companies like Custom Cottages Inc., The Fish House Store, Ice Castle Fish Houses Manufacturing, and Zachmeier Mfg. Inc. sell parts for do-it-yourselfers or custom package ice houses.

As I noted earlier, the main downside to these huts is that moving them requires more effort and towing. This doesn't facilitate a mobile-style of fishing, but permanent shelters do deliver other advantages. My friends who own permanent shelters like them because they're great for introducing their children and families to ice fishing together in a comfortable environment.

The other main advantage is that permanent shelters make for quick and easy outings with friends or spouses. Since the shelter is already on the ice and equipped for fishing, you don't need to load a vehicle with a lot of gear or pull a hut out to a fishing spot. Instead, you can drive directly to the house, unlock the door, fire up a propane heater or wood stove – even

Ray Allard, the author's father, emerges from a permanent shelter with a Northern-Ontario prize, a whitefish.

cook a meal on a portable stove – and settle in for some relaxing fishing. Even if there's not much biting, being able to share fishing experiences with others is sometimes just as rewarding as catching impressive numbers of fish or trophies.

Be sure to check your state or provincial fishing regulations, as there are often registration and removal deadlines for these fish houses.

OTHER OPTIONS

Before I move off the subject of ice shelters, there are two other items worth mentioning: buckets and sleds. Like countless other anglers, I've spent hours sitting hunched over on a bucket on the ice. A basic 6-gallon pail can be used to carry gear and then either inverted or outfitted with a specialized add-on cushion for a seat. Although it may appear archaic and lacks the luxury of some of the shelter options, my friends and I have a different term for it...

Kickin' it old school.

When I get a phone call during a spell of mild weather and the voice on the other end says, "Don't bother bringing your shelter; we're going old school," I know to bring my bucket and to be prepared for a lot of walking. As much as I love my flip-over shelter, buckets simplify fishing. I can carry my bucket and most of my stuff in one hand, my rods in a case in the other, and store the remaining gear in my trusty backpack.

Sometimes we might go old school because we're car-pooling to a distant destination and we simply don't have the space. In other cases, it might be because we're going to a lake that can't be accessed with ATVs and pulling a shelter would be exhausting. Folding chairs are another option, but it's tough to beat the low cost and carrying capacity of a simple bucket.

A word of warning, however: if you're planning to sit and fish on a pail all day, it's paramount to dress properly and carry extra layers. Until recently I wouldn't have recommended this approach for cold temperatures; however, with the advancement in ice fishing outwear (such as Snosuit) it's amazing how well these garments will keep you comfortable. In high winds, however, bring a portable. The shelter prevents your line from being blown around, dramatically increasing your ability to maintain feel on light jigs and detect faint hits.

In addition to buckets, small sleds are also practical. I've already mentioned how useful sleds are as part of a flip-over shelter. When you're carrying only buckets to sit on, loading up a lightweight sled with an auger and heavier items is an easy way to transport equipment.

Stores carry a variety of sleds. Some ice fishing sleds are designed to be connected to snow machines or ATVs, so their weight makes them tough to pull on foot over long distances, especially in thick snow. There are others, however, which are designed to be pulled by hand, such as

The Shappell Jet Sled gives anglers a light-weight option for transporting essential gear.

Shappell Corporation's Jet Sled or Otter Outdoors' Wild Mini Sled. Children's snow sleds are an alternative, but they're often not as deep, so it's best to secure gear using bungee cords.

FINISHING TOUCHES

Once you decide on which type of ice shelter is best for your fishing style, you can have some fun outfitting it with accessories. Flip-over, cabin, and permanent huts lend themselves to customization particularly well. I've already alluded to some items you can use to outfit your shelter, namely covers, runners, and tow hitches, but they're worth revisiting. Again, do yourself a favor and buy a cover. It'll keep snow and slush out during travel, but also secure items inside and prevent them from falling out. Runners installed on the bottom of a shelter make it easier to pull shelters and protect the sled from wear. Tow bars are used to connect portable shelters to snow machines or ATVs and are a legal requirement if pulling shelters with motorized vehicles in many instances.

For the last several ice seasons, I've been engaged in a friendly competition with my ice fishing chums vying to see who can create the supreme ice fishing machine by customizing a portable shelter. We've

A tow bar makes for safe shelter towing with a snow machine. A cover's important as well to keep snow from collecting in the sled base but also prevents objects from falling out during travel.

found that there's no limit to what you can do. Here are just a few shelter outfitting tips and tricks.

- **Permanent Lights** - Several companies make long, flexible tubes filled with LED lights, such as the 3-foot Light Rope by Clam Corporation. The lights are mounted on shelter poles with plastic zip ties, providing excellent overhead lighting. After installing the ties, use sandpaper or a file to smooth the edges of the ties to reduce the chances of tearing the shelter's tent fabric. Power source options include stand-alone batteries or through a 12-volt source like the battery used in a portable sonar.
- **Hangers** - Designed to fit over the shelter's frame on the inside of the hut, hangers can hold a variety of accessories. Use them to dry a pair of gloves, hold a hat, or hang a fleece vest. Low in cost, these handy items help keep your gear off the ice, out of your sled, and easily within reach.
- **Rod Holders** - Installing removable rod holders for your shelter is a good idea. Inexpensive, they keep your rod secure and out of the way when busy with other tasks. Otherwise you're likely to lay down the rod somewhere, which can boost the chances of an accidental break.
- **Foam Floor** - Use flexible, closed-cell foam to line the tub of your shelter. The padding is less slippery than plastic and helps prevent things from sliding around.
- **Screw-in Eyes** - Installed on the inside of your shelter tub, these are great for securing bungee cords to hold items in place.
- **Coolers and Crates** - To create extra storage space and compartmentalize their shelters a few anglers I know use plastic milk crates and coolers. Secure milk crates with plastic zip ties to reduce movement. Coolers provide dry storage and also serve double duty as a second seat.
- **Extra Rope** - To make pulling portable shelters and sleds an easier task, tie on an additional few feet of extra rope or simply replace the factory provided one with a longer length. This allows you to pull in a more upright and comfortable manner by crossing the rope over your shoulder.
- **Anchors** - Ice anchors keep your hut in place when you're fishing on minimally covered ice on windy days. There are two main options: anchors that screw into the ice or those that are secured in

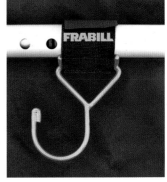
Frabill's Shelter Hanger.

partly drilled ice holes. These come in handy – I've seen my fair share of anglers get out of a shelter only to be spotted moments later chasing their wind-blown hut down an icy lake.

Wrap Up

Sheltering yourself from winter's harsh elements and being comfortable are important when ice fishing. Portable, permanent, or rustic pail-and-sled combinations are all options when it comes to hitting the hard water. Each has strengths and weaknesses, depending on the situation, your budget, and the style of fishing you prefer. When starting out, a bucket or basic portable shelter is a great way to gain experience. Something to keep in mind when buying a portable shelter is you get what you pay for. Spending the extra dollars will likely result in a longer lasting product built with better material. I didn't mind paying more for my portable because it meant I'd be sitting comfortably with a cushioned seat and a backrest. It's been well worth it, especially on long days sitting in my hut, staring at my electronics in search of big fish.

A flip-over shelter blocked the wind, helping the author finesse this crappie.

5

ELECTRONICS

ELECTRONICS

Sonars, underwater cameras, and global positioning systems (GPS) are the most common electronics used in ice fishing. Hard-core anglers consider these devices – particularly portable sonar units – indispensible. A sonar gives you water depth, tracks the location of your lure in the water column, and displays if there are fish in the area. A camera's video monitor lets you see what's beneath you, making it a great tool for sight fishing. A GPS unit boosts your ability to navigate to a lake as well as on it. You can mark and save fishing hotspots as waypoints to return to another time. Used together, these technological gadgets give you useful data about the underwater world. Ace ice anglers use electronics to position themselves on the best fishing spots and employ these tools to tweak their angling strategies to get fish biting.

When first starting out, you don't need electronics to catch fish. Yet, as you get more involved in ice fishing (and I'm hopeful you will), these instruments will accelerate your learning and make you a better angler. In this chapter, you'll get the run-down on the latest in ice fishing electronics and how to use them to catch more fish.

SONAR

In open water angling, most boats are equipped with a sonar unit. In the previous chapter, I compared portable ice huts to fishing boats. Not surprisingly, more and more ice anglers are including sonar as part of their hard-water fishing gear. Today, portable sonar units specifically designed for ice fishing are available at various price points from Humminbird, Lowrance, MarCum Technologies, Versa Electronics, and Vexilar. Considering the value these units deliver on the ice, it's a wonder why you wouldn't own one if you can afford it. Having a basic understanding of how sonar operates will help you appreciate the advantages these instru-

Ken Whiting carefully watches a Humminbird Ice 55 Flasher as he works his bait a few inches off bottom.

ments provide but will also give you insight on how to interpret the data they display when ice fishing.

How Sonar Works

The word sonar derives from the first letters of "SOund NAvigation and Ranging." A fishing sonar unit has four main parts: transmitter, transducer, receiver, and display. The technology centers on the device's ability to send sound energy into the water and measure the amount of time it takes to bounce off the bottom (or other objects) and return to the source, creating an image on the screen. As sound energy travels through water at a consistent speed, a sonar can calculate bottom depth and the general depth of other objects in the water. This sequence repeats itself several times a second, giving users a continuous display of what's within the sonar's cone. This is a rather simplistic overview, but a few points in particular are worth highlighting in more detail as they relate to specific ice fishing situations.

Cone Angles

Cone angle is a term used to describe the pattern of the sound energy a transducer emits. Understanding cone angle helps you interpret your unit's display. As sound travels deeper, the area it covers widens. The area a cone angle covers is influenced by the transducer's beam angle. For example, an 8-degree transducer has a smaller area of coverage than a 12-degree transducer.

When it comes to ice fishing, a larger-angled transducer, like a 19 degree, tends to be better for shallow water situations with minimal weed cover (under 30 feet) or when you're targeting suspended fish. The downside to a large angle is that you're more likely to pick up interference from other sonar units if you're fishing close to other anglers. To combat this most companies have different settings to reduce cross-talk interference.

A smaller cone is often better for deeper water fishing as it concentrates the beam's power in a smaller area. A 12-degree transducer is a good option up to 45 feet and a 8- or 9-degree transducer for anything deeper than this. Smaller cone sizes are also better suited to fishing around drop-off structures like break lines or points, as they are less likely to create a dead zone. A dead zone is an area within the unit's cone angle that is not displayed. This occurs because a sonar unit will mark bottom

MarCum Technologies LX-5 Ice Sonar

Dave Bennett studies his Vexilar's display as he works a mid-lake hump for whitefish.

based on the highest point of contact. Dead zones frequently happen when targeting fish on a steep slope or when fishing near a large boulder or log. Lastly, a small area of coverage will also help reduce clutter when fishing in weeds and help you spot moving fish between plant signals.

To satisfy the needs of serious, multi-species anglers, some companies make dual degree transducers. This lets anglers switch from wide to narrow beams depending on water depth and conditions. Vexilar and Humminbird sell a dual 9- and 19-degree transducer, while MarCum has an 8- or 20-degree option. However, Vexilar (who has a significant portion of the market share) sells more straight 12-degree transducers than any other transducer for two reasons. The first is that a straight 12-degree transducer crystal is up to 20% more sensitive than a dual beam and the 12-degree beam angle tends to be one that performs in nearly all fishing situations, making it an excellent all-round choice.

Displays

When it comes to portable ice fishing sonars, there are a few types of displays to choose from. Let's begin with flashers.

Flasher Units

Flasher units, like those produced by Vexilar, Humminbird and MarCum, are very popular with ice anglers. Vexilar in particular has built a well-deserved reputation for high-quality ice electronics, with a variety of portable units available with different features.

Flashers have a circular display. In operation, a flasher will contain multi-colored lines of light at different locations on its display. The location of the lights are then cross-referenced with the depth markings on the face of the unit to determine the whereabouts of bottom, weeds, your lure, and fish. It may sound complicated, but you'll quickly get the hang of reading these units. To familiarize yourself with your unit's features, be sure to read your owner's manual. If you purchased a Vexilar, take the time to view their training DVD included with every flasher.

One major advantage of flashers is their displays are in real time, meaning that fish or your lure's movements immediately show up on the screen. When a fish comes in to inspect a bait, you get instantaneous feedback on its positioning and the strength of its signal. This helps you tweak your lure presentation to coax fish to bite. Flashers also perform well in extremely cold temperatures.

Most of today's flashers are three-color models. Color depicts the strength of the echo signal, providing critical details on what's beneath you. For example, Vexilar's three-color signals are as follows: green is the weakest; orange is moderate, and red is the strongest signal. Pay attention

The Humminbird Ice-55 Flasher features a 6-color fiber optic display, plus a centre LCD display that automatically adjusts the depth scale.

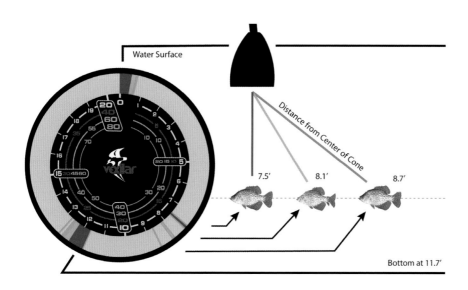

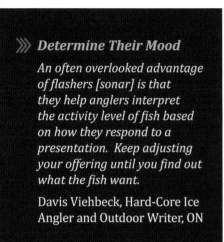

to the different types of colors when fishing as they'll help you interpret what's going on below the ice.

As you can see in the illustration on the previous page, the bottom depth is 11.7 feet, and the target species are crappie – notorious suspenders. One is stationed at 7.5 feet and displays as a bright red mark. This fish is right in the centre of the cone angle (where the signal's strength is the strongest). The other two fish are increasingly further from center and are displayed as an orange mark at 8.1 feet and a green mark one at 8.7 feet.

If you were ice fishing these crappies, this is a likely scenario with active fish. You'd drop your jig down to about 6 feet. The bait would display as a thin, green mark which would quickly get bit by the red-mark fish that swam up from 7.5 feet. Lowering your jig a second time, your best bet would be to again stop at 6 feet down. After some jigging it's likely the fish at 8.1 feet may become interested and its signal will begin to flicker and move. On the display, the fish appears to be swimming up to your bait because the mark climbs from 8.1 towards 6 feet. The signal also gets stronger as it approaches. Although the display portrays the fish as rising to take the bait, it's actually swimming in from the side as it was suspended at 7.5 but positioned further from the centre of the cone. The same can be said about green fish signal at 8.7 feet.

This example illustrates the usefulness of color displays to determine fish whereabouts within the cone angle coverage area beneath you. It also highlights that it's good practice to jig baits a few feet above a fish, as it may be out to the side of the cone angle.

What's interesting is that through the use of your flasher, you'll begin to learn how different fish behave and are displayed on the screen. You'll learn to recognized the slow, sauntering flickers of suspended neutral mood crappie, the telltale off-bottom sprints and retreats of pint-sized perch, and the strong accelerating signal of an aggressive lake trout.

Zoom Settings

High-end flashers have a split-screen zoom function allowing you to magnify the bottom 6- or 12-feet, while some units allow you to magnify any section of the water column. Bottom zoom is useful when fish are holding tight to a lake or river's floor. This function magnifies the fish and bottom, giving you more detail. When hole-hopping different depths and using bottom zoom, you need to return the flasher to the normal setting when

Properly tuning your sonar on the ice is important for accurate readings.

you first put the transducer down a new hole. Once it locks in on bottom, switch to zoom mode. This produces the most precise reading.

Type of Bottom

Flashers display hard and soft bottom areas differently. When using a Vexilar flasher for example, soft bottom areas are displayed as wide marks with some red mixed with plenty of orange and green. The latter two colors reflect a weaker echo, as the bottom is absorbing sound energy. On the other hand, a rock bottom that reflects sound better is represented by a thinner red mark. This information can be advantageous when looking for specific habitat. Hard rock structures can be the ticket for walleye and lake trout looking to ambush smaller fish. Softer bottom spots appeal to perch, crappie, and sunfish dining on the invertebrates inhabiting this spongy zone. Transitions between hard and soft bottoms also concentrate fish, so compare readings between different holes.

Jason Mitchell, a North Dakota Fishing Guide and Rod Designer, takes his Vexilar use a step further. He'll set his sonar to a much deeper range than the water depth, such as using the 0-80 foot setting in 30 feet of water. On this setting Mitchell looks for echo signals. The harder the bottom the more likely a third or even fourth echo. When fishing expansive flats for perch, he uses this technique to look for subtle soft to hard bottom changes, like rock piles, that are magnets for jumbos.

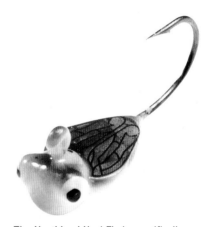
The Northland Hexi Fly is specifically engineered to return a consistent, well-defined sonar signal so you can focus on hooking fish without worrying about loosing sight of your jig.

A Word on Gain

On flasher units, the gain (i.e., sensitivity) setting helps you control the strength of the signal you see on the display. Once you establish the depth, adjust the gain so that your lure shows up as weak signal, but is continuously displayed when jigged. A common mistake of some anglers new to using flashers is to turn the gain up too high. This results in a busy, cluttered screen and makes it difficult to discern what's a fish and what's not.

You'll often need to increase the gain when fishing in deep water. Current can also push your lure to the periphery of the cone angle, which is another instance where increasing your gain may be necessary to see your bait. As you become more proficient at interpreting the unit, you may also crank the gain at times to get more data, such as suspended fish on the edges of your cone angle, but in most cases, keeping the gain set between zero to about 35% will do.

Other Portable Sonar Options

Flashers aren't the only players in the ice fishing sonar game and two other products deserve mentioning.

One is the Lowrance X67C IceMachine Fishfinder. This sonar features a flat, color TFT screen with different display options for users. One option is a flasher view, where data is displayed around a circular dial display (see photo). The other main option is the full sonar chart display. In this setting the water column is pictured vertically on this scrolling screen. When ice fishing using the chart display, the bottom takes on a continuous line (as you're not changing depths). When you jig your bait, the lure and any fish that follow will move up and down on the screen as it's updated, creating a display of various lines. One reason some anglers prefer these units to flashers is that the display will temporarily capture history on its scrolling screen. This allows you to see the depth a fish swam from to hit a lure, and how aggressive it was (according to the angle of the line). Lowrance notes these units perform well in cold temperatures (to -4 degrees Fahrenheit). The reason is the unit's color TFT display is comprised of individual pixels. Each pixel is "fired" by it's own transistor resulting in a fluid and flowing display without dimming or slowing down in colder temperatures. It features automatic or manual depth range settings.

Another option is Versa Electronics' ShowDown Digital Fish Finder with a liquid crystal display (LCD). Lightweight, compact, and easy to use this product has a thin rectangular screen, mimicking the water column. It doesn't have a scrolling display but rather shows fish, lures, and bottom as grey to black bands. As you jig your lure, it rises up and down in the thin vertical display. The ShowDown features a heated ice mode which keeps the crystals moving at high-speed, even in extremely cold conditions. It also boasts 10-level noise reduction and an automatic depth range setting.

The two units above contain a variety of features and menu options. Increasing the sensitivity setting to display more signals could be compared to turning up the gain in a flasher unit. They also have adjustable zoom features as well.

What to Look for in a Portable Unit

Regardless of what type of display you choose, there are a couple of features you should look for when purchasing a unit. First and foremost, you'll want an ice-fishing specific sonar that is compact and easy to operate. Most portables today are sold with a hard plastic case or frame to secure the unit, cables, transducer, and battery. In particular, the sonar case should have a transducer holder. Fragility increases in the cold, and too many knocks over time will damage the transducer, weakening its signal and lessening its accuracy. A zippered soft-pack carry bag is useful

Versa Electronics ShowDown

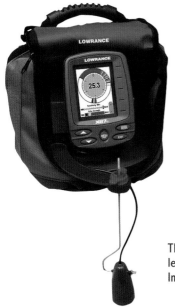

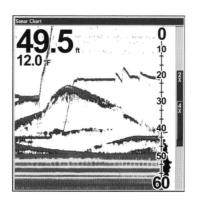

The Lowrance X67C IceMachine in Ice Flasher view on left. The right image shows the full sonar chart view. Images: Navico, www.lowrance.com

Digging for Knowledge »

Many manufacturer websites have FAQs, tutorials, and other resources providing sonar information well beyond what's in the owner's manual. Studying this information will make you a more sophisticated sonar user.

Photo: Stu McKay

to keep snow and ice from collecting on the plastic frame holding the sonar, battery, and wiring.

Ice fishing combos will also include a holder to align the transducer correctly. It's critical to proper operation that the transducer hangs straight in the hole. This is accomplished by either a float or a supporting arm depending on the sonar unit you're using.

Hand-Held Depth Sonar

These simple, compact devices are designed to show depth exclusively on a digital, numeric display. They can take readings through clear ice, although you may need to wet the ice first for a decent bond (this trick works with other sonar transducers too). With the unit on the ice or in an ice hole, simply press a button and read the digital display for depth. These small units don't give you anywhere near as much information as flashers or LCD sonars, but they're convenient on remote trips where weight and size restrictions may prevent you from bringing a lot of gear. Two of these products are the Vexilar LPS-1 Digital Handheld Depth Sounder and the MarCum LX-i Hand-Held Digital Sonar.

The Vexilar LPS-1 Digital Handheld Depth Sounder provides a digital read out of the depth.

UNDERWATER CAMERAS

For the inquisitive angler, an underwater camera packs plenty of rewards – letting you explore the aquatic environment. Cameras give you an image of the structures and cover you're fishing, like the layout of rocks on bottom or the health or species of weeds beneath you. They also provide plenty of information about fish behavior. After a bit of time with a camera, you'll start to learn how to interpret the posture and movement of fish. It's also a learning experience to use a camera to watch how lures behave beneath the ice when jigged. You can see how the faintest jiggles of the hand can impart just enough action to coax an on-looking panfish into biting. Lastly, cameras add an element of entertainment to angling. When taking children or new anglers on the ice, cameras can help hold their attention and engage them in fishing.

The set-up of an underwater viewing system for ice fishing is straightforward. A small camera is connected to a cable, which in turn is plugged in to a display. To use the unit, simply turn it on, lower the camera into the water and watch the screen. When you're preparing to fish for a while in the same area, drill a separate hole exclusively for the camera. This lessens the odds of fish tangling in the cord when you fight them.

Camera Considerations

Aqua-Vu and MarCum Technologies make portable underwater cameras available for ice fishing. However, there are a number of feature options to keep in mind when you're purchasing an underwater camera.

Cameras are available with traditional television-type screens, but LCD monitors are entering the scene. Although the majority of screens are black and white, some models, such as the VS825c by MarCum Technologies, have color.

When selecting a camera, spend some time setting it up, unraveling the cord, and then preparing it for storage and transport as you would when ice fishing. Some designs make for easier operation than others.

A short cord makes it easy for Brendan Mark to remove the transducer from the hole while playing a fish.

Underwater cameras provide a real-life picture of what lies beneath the ice.

Remember that you'll be doing this in the cold. The fewer screws, snaps, and other steps you need to go through to set up or dismantle a unit the better. Cameras should feature a lighting system to help you see underwater. Although even with lights, murky water won't feature the same visibility as clear water for underwater viewing.

A SONAR OR A CAMERA?

A question I often get from beginner ice anglers is "should I buy a sonar or a camera?" This is really a comparing apples to oranges scenario. My answer is to buy a sonar first and here's why:

Sonar units work in clear to murky water, at any depth, in day and night, and they display data from the entire water column within its cone angle. Cameras are much more limited. Water clarity impacts camera visibility and you'll see very little in murky water or at night. Plus, you won't see fish swimming behind or above the camera lens.

With cameras you'll also need to lower enough cable to reach the depth you want to view and it takes time to fine-tune the camera's direction in a horizontal position. Worth noting is you can adjust the camera lens on many units to point down, called down-viewing, which gives you an overhead perspective on what's visible beneath the lens. Hole-hopping is much easier with a sonar as you simply need to get the transducer wet.

As previously mentioned, cameras do offer some benefits, like observing fish behavior or scouting cover, but you should be aware of their limitations (i.e., water clarity and cords). Sonar, however, is a more encompassing technology that can be used in any ice fishing situation. Simply put, you get a lot more out of a sonar than you do with an underwater camera.

So, if I can only take one, I'll grab my sonar. But being a visual learner, I've found using cameras have helped me understand what's happening beneath the ice, whether it's learning the different action of lures or seeing what structure or cover caused fish to inhabit a specific area.

GLOBAL POSITIONING SYSTEM (GPS) UNITS

GPS units add an incredible dimension of precision to your ice angling game. This technology can identify your location anywhere in the world within a few yards or meters by gathering data from satellites orbiting the earth.

Using the internal memory of a GPS unit, you can store waypoints to mark spots such as a mid-lake hump or lake access roads. You can plot and store a route or leave a breadcrumb trail for safe navigation. This is helpful when travelling long distances on snow machines or ATVs. They can be just as handy on foot. I recall an early January outing several years ago where a combination of light rain and mild temperatures made for extremely foggy conditions in the afternoon. Although we knew the lake fairly well, having a GPS containing our trail for the day and a waypoint marking where we accessed the ice made it much easier to return to our vehicles.

Hand-held GPS units are quite popular with ice anglers. They are easily stored in a pocket without too much weight or bulk. There are some other instruments, such as the LCD Lowrance 522c Ice Machine, that also include GPS as well. If you use this unit in your boat in the summer, you can mark all of your favorite spots and then refer to the data when using it on the ice. I've also seen anglers mount these 5-inch screens to the dash of their snow machines for navigation purposes alone.

Choose a GPS unit with a multi-media card slot. Although many units come with pre-loaded information, multi-media card slots deliver plug-and-play capability with map chips containing electronic charts, like those by Navionics. For example, let's say you're heading out to fish

Steve Barnett uses his Lowrance iFINDER™ GPS unit to determine the location of a drop-off.

Dave Bennett gets his bearings while plotting his next move on Lake of the Woods.

an unknown area for walleye. You own a hand-held GPS unit and have a media card with marine charts for the lake. Using the depth-contour data, you can pinpoint areas you'd like to fish (such as a mid-depth hump) and navigate on the ice to these underwater structures. Where this technology exists, it can greatly improve your on-ice efficiency. For smaller lakes off the beaten track, this level of detail isn't often available, but you can still use a GPS unit to supplement road or topographic maps for navigation purposes. As you discover more spots, store them in the unit so you can easily pinpoint them on your next outing.

In most instances, you get what you pay for when choosing a GPS unit. Color screens deliver improved read-outs and assist in your ability to process the information the unit displays. Fishing-specific units are often waterproof (something well worth investing in). Higher-end models also deliver larger internal memory capacities.

Wrap Up

Electronics add another dimension of precision to ice fishing. Over time, you'll learn to interpret sonar signals and you'll acquire knowledge about fish behavior by using an underwater camera. Integrating GPS technology into your fishing system will enhance your ability to scout and return to spots. Together, these instruments increase your overall knowledge when it comes to fish whereabouts beneath the ice.

Remember, all electronics require a power source. For smaller items like handheld GPS units, be sure to bring spare batteries and keep them warm. Most sonars and cameras feature robust 12v batteries that, if properly cared for, should last a full day of fishing. When you return home, let batteries reach room temperature and then charge them immediately to keep their reserve capacity at its maximum and to ensure the longest lifespan possible.

As a beginning ice angler, you don't need electronics. They really enhance your fishing experience, however. If you're unsure about investing in this equipment, consider borrowing a unit from a friend or asking another angler to show you how their devices function. A lot of fishing electronics tend to sell themselves better on the ice than in a store.

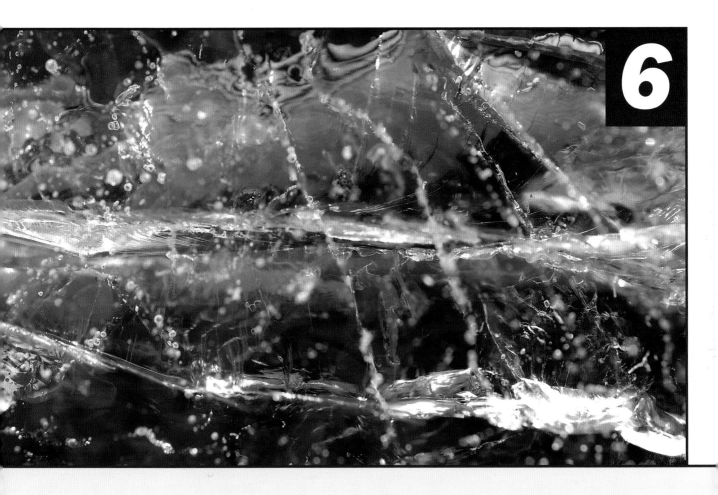

6

SAFETY

ICE FISHING SAFETY

In the previous chapters, I've discussed the basic gear you'll need to start ice fishing and how some sophisticated tools can help you progress as an angler. As you've seen, there's no shortage of "stuff" available to help you become a more comfortable, efficient, and effective angler on the ice. Of course, you still need to put in the effort to find the fish and tempt them into biting. After all, isn't that the fun of it in the first place? In the second part of this book, I'll discuss species-specific tactics in detail, but before moving on, it's important to touch on some safety information not yet covered.

No book on ice fishing would be complete without a section on safety. Truth be told, today there are limited activities that are risk-free. The cold reality is that ice is never 100% safe and there's always an element of the unknown when you stand on frozen water. Also remember that you can never judge the strength of ice by its appearance alone as there are several interrelated factors that influence its strength. Understanding and respecting conditions and adopting a cautious approach are the best

things you can do to help keep your outings as safe as possible.

In this chapter, I'll cover information I've acquired over the years related to ice and ice fishing safety. Ice fishing is a fun and exciting winter activity, but no matter how well the fish are biting, safety should always be in the forefront of your mind. This chapter is in no way meant to deter you from enjoying the adventures of hard-water angling. On the contrary – I hope it either re-emphasizes information you already know or shares some new practices so your future outings are that much safer and enjoyable.

ICE SAFETY

Ice Thickness

Ice thickness is vital when it comes to determining the amount of weight that can be supported. A multitude of factors impact the quality of ice that is formed, but little snow and consistent freezing temperatures create the best conditions for ice to form and thicken. Temperature fluctuations, freeze-thaw cycles, and heavy snow during early winter can create layered ice, which may not support as much weight as clear ice of the same thickness.

The strongest ice is new, clear black, blue, or green ice. The following rough guidelines are endorsed by various North American safety organizations with the caveat that "no ice is ever 100% safe."
- 4" (10cm) minimum for ice fishing, walking, cross-country skiing
- 5" (12cm) one snow machine or ATV
- 8 – 12" (20 – 30cm) one car or small pick-up
- 12 – 15" (30 – 38cm) one medium truck or van

Again, to reiterate, the above guidelines apply to new, solid, clear ice under ideal conditions. Honeycombed or layered ice will not support as much weight as clear ice. It's simply not as strong. Here are some other ice safety tips.

Ice Safety Tips

Before heading out for a fish, check with local authorities about the thickness of the ice. Police, local media, tackle shops, fishing resorts or ice hut operators, as well as snow machine clubs are decent sources of information. At first and late ice, this is an especially important step.

The author uses a chisel to check ice quality and thickness. Note the auto-inflating PFD.

Wear a flotation suit, especially when unsure of ice conditions. In Chapter 1, I described in detail how these suits work. To recap briefly, they provide thermal insulation and can reduce the effects of cold shock should you fall through the ice. The suit's flotation properties also helps to keep your head above water, reducing the chances of drowning. This also betters your odds of being able to perform a self-rescue and pull yourself out of the water. Opting for a flotation jacket instead of a full body suit is another option, as is wearing a personal flotation device (PFD).

When you arrive at a fishing area, carefully inspect the shoreline. If there's a gap between the ice and the shore, it's best to stay off the ice. If the ice is frozen up to the shore and looks relatively safe, go forward and start testing it. Also, don't assume that if other anglers are fishing or if you spot snow machine or cross-country ski tracks that the ice is safe. Tracks can sometimes be a false indicator and following them can sometimes get you into trouble, so unless you know the area, always check the ice yourself.

Using a chisel is one way to test ice thickness (see Chapter 3), particularly during early and late ice periods. Use it like a walking stick, hitting the ice in front of you to test its thickness. Another option is drilling a hole and measuring the ice. As long as there's enough clear, solid ice, continue this process every few meters as you walk to your fishing spot.

Avoid pressure cracks as they are natural weak points in the ice. On thin ice (a minimum four inches – anything less and you shouldn't risk it), don't walk in tight groups but spread out to distribute your weight evenly. Remember, ice thickness is rarely uniform so remain cautious. If you detect thin ice back up and retrace your steps back the way you came (as you know that ice is safe).

Be mindful of and avoid areas where there are currents, as they have an impact on how ice forms and its thickness. Rivers, inlets and outlets, underwater springs, and narrow areas are zones where currents might create anomalies in the ice, resulting in a non-uniform sheet. Also, ice thickness varies throughout a lake or a river as well as from one water body to the next in different locales.

Avoid going out on the ice alone in dark and/or stormy conditions. Reduced visibility increases the risks associated with travelling on ice. Of course, twilight and night can yield some of the best fishing, so be responsible at night and pack a flashlight in your tackle bag. Use a GPS or compass to navigate safely back to shore as well.

If driving on the ice, keep the following tips in mind: Use established access points and ice roads. Unlock your doors, unbuckle your seat belt, and roll down the windows so you can quickly evacuate the vehicle should it break through. Turn all lights on. Keep plenty of space between yourself and the next vehicle to spread out weight. Drive slowly. This allows you to watch for pressure cracks and other obstacles, but also reduces the size and intensity of the underwater wake your vehicle creates beneath the ice. Avoid typical bad ice areas, such as the narrows of a lake.

Lastly, always leave an itinerary with someone. Include cell phone numbers, where you're fishing, who you're fishing with, and when you plan on being back.

ICE RESCUE TIPS

Play your cards right when deciding whether or not to set foot on the ice and exercise caution and ideally you'll never encounter the situation of falling through the ice. The fact remains, however, that it's always a possibility, no matter how slim the odds. There are different theories out there about whether a group of untrained people should attempt to rescue someone or wait for help from professionals. This is easy to consider if you're fishing in a community spot near cities and towns with appropriate emergency response personnel, but I'd feel remiss if I did not report what I've learned over the years by talking with experts and personal research about rescue techniques when that help isn't available.

Increasing melt-water run off during March quickly opened up this area on a river.

Self Rescue

John Blaicher, a North American ice safety consultant for 25 years, has conducted ice safety and cold-water rescue demonstrations across the continent. Here's what he explained to me about the steps of self-rescue.

"What kills most people who fall in cold water is not hypothermia – but drowning – because they can't keep their head above water," says Blaicher. "In the first minute, the goal is to get one's breathing under control as the body experiences cold shock," he says. The initial plunge in cold water results in breathing difficulties, beginning with a large involuntary gasp and hyperventilation effect. Staying calm, controlling your breathing, and calling for help should be the first things you do before attempting to get out.

"Once breathing is under control, the next ten minutes are critical to use your big motor muscles and try to get out of the water. In cold water, the brain sends signals to redirect blood flow to the body's core and starts

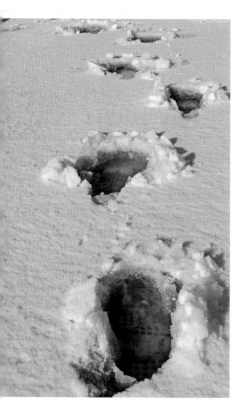

to shut down blood flow to the extremities of the arms and legs," explains Blaicher. Wearing flotation garments (like a PFD) and being buoyant dramatically improves one's ability to breathe, swim, and lift oneself out of the water, but time is of the essence.

To get out of the water and onto safe ice, do the following. Kick vigorously into a horizontal, floating position. Swim in the direction you fell in; this ice already supported your weight. At the edge, reach forward onto the ice, gently lift your torso to drain some water from your clothing and reduce your weight. Having ice picks gives you extra traction.

Next, kick vigorously into a horizontal position; thrust yourself up onto the ice like a seal using your arms and legs to propel yourself forward. Do not stand up. Raise your upper body so water drains from your clothing to reduce weight. Look ahead to make sure you are going in the right direction. Remain on your stomach, crawling forward. Staying flat evenly distributes weight, lessening your chances of falling through again. Don't stand up until you reach ground or unquestionably solid ice.

If you are unable to get out of the water, the clock is ticking. "In ice cold water, the average person has upwards of 60 minutes of survival time before the heart stops or unconsciousness sets in due to hypothermia," says Blaicher, who cautions there are many influencing factors that affect this estimate.

If you do make it out of the water, Blaicher suggests getting to shelter you can find in less than 30 minutes or remaining where you are and protecting yourself from the elements. In each case, ring out wet garments and change into dry clothing if available, which is why it's good practice to carry a spare set of clothes in your vehicle. If you are seeking shelter, keep moving to increase heat production, but don't exhaust yourself. If you are staying put, wrap yourself in some kind of wind break or insulation. If you can, get off the ice and build a fire to warm yourself.

Rescuing Another

It's best to leave ice rescues to trained professionals. Call 911 should you spot an angler who's fallen through the ice. However, in remote areas when time is of the essence, the following procedures are recommended to assist someone struggling to get out of the ice.

Your primary objective should always be maintaining your own safety. Stay on safe ice and keep your distance from the opening. You should also keep your centre of gravity as low as possible – lie down if you can. Your first step should be trying to talk the individual through the self-rescue steps above. If they're unable to free themselves, find something to extend to the victim that they can grab on to and be helped out of the water. I take the throw rope out of my boat come winter and carry it my ice shelter for this exact purpose. An extension cord is another option (just make sure its unplugged). It's unlikely someone in frigid water will have the strength to keep a firm grip on a wet rope, so make a large loop that the victim can put over their head and under their arms or elbows so you can pull them out. If you can't find anything to throw, the other option is extending something, such as a ladder, a long branch, or an aluminum boat. These items are often common on cottage shorelines. Never make direct contact with the victim or you risk being pulled in and quickly becoming another person that needs rescuing.

SAFETY GEAR

In earlier chapters I listed gear in terms of clothing, equipment, and fishing tackle. This section gives an overview of what safety equipment you should carry with you when you're ice fishing.

Get a Grip: Cleats and Picks

Two important ice safety items are ice cleats and ice picks. Cleats are designed to fit over your boots and provide extra traction when walking on slippery ice. These inexpensive devices are a must during slick ice conditions. Bare, wind-blown or puddle-rich ice can be extremely slippery and I've seen my fair share of ice anglers not wearing cleats quickly go from a vertical to a horizontal position, even when treading with caution.

Ice picks – also called claws – help you get a grip during the life-threatening situation of falling through the ice. There are several brands on the market; all feature handles attached to a sharp pick. Instead of attempting to grip slippery ice and snow with cold, wet hands, picks help you anchor and pull yourself out of the ice. Handles are designed to fit together and cover the pick points when not in use so you don't have to worry about puncturing your clothing with them during storage. Handles are often joined by a cord, so when walking on the ice, simply loop the line around your neck to keep the picks within reach. Always carry these items on the ice.

Cleats, like HT Enterprises Sure Grip All Purpose Treads, improve traction on bare ice conditions.

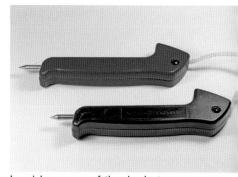

Ice picks are one of the simplest, cheapest, and most important pieces of safety gear that you can carry.

First Aid and Safety Kit

A first aid kit should be a mandatory piece of gear you carry with you whenever you ice fish. It won't take up a lot of space and the overall weight is miniscule in comparison to all the other fishing items you bring. For less than $25, you can assemble your own kit or buy one from an outdoor store with antiseptic, bandages, tape, scissors, and so on. Store the kit in a waterproof bag to keep the contents protected.

Beyond a first aid kit, assemble a small safety survival kit and keep it on your person or in your shelter. Contents of a kit should include: waterproof matches or a lighter, a fire starter kit, a whistle, compass, and a knife. An energy bar or two, chocolate, and a space blanket are also good ideas. All these items can fit in a small sealed sandwich bag. It might seem overkill to carry this stuff to a community hole, but by keeping gear on your person at all times, you'll be prepared on the off chance that you get stuck in the woods overnight or need to build a fire and take shelter in an emergency situation. It's unlikely you'll ever need to use the kit, but it pays to be prepared, especially if you're a back-country explorer.

Spare Clothes

In addition to carrying the above safety articles, pack a bag with spare clothes and bring it on your trips. I put one in my vehicle at the start of the ice season and leave it there all winter. The spare clothes are there as a precaution in case someone gets wet and needs to change. I've never been out on an outing when someone has fallen through the ice completely, but I've seen friends get soakers by unknowingly stepping in unmarked ice holes. Whether full immersion or a wet foot, spare clothes come in handy to get out of heat-depriving wet garments quickly.

AUGERS AND BLADES

On the topic of ice safety, it's worth pointing out that augers can do a fair amount of harm if not handled properly. Proper handling begins by always keeping the blades covered when not in use. When removing the blade cover, do so slowly and carefully. "Accidents happen when you work too fast," was said to me by a foreman at one of my university summer jobs. It's a great piece of wisdom well suited to handling ice augers – or any powered machine for that matter. Again, remember to tuck-in loose

Wearing picks around one's neck is good practice to ensure they're accessible in the case of an accidental dunking.

clothing or anything hanging, like belts or lanyards, as you drill. Stray items can get caught in an auger and can quickly turn an ordinary scene into a dangerous one.

FOOD AND WATER

What do food and water have to do with ice fishing safety? Quite a bit, actually. Bringing enough food and eating right prevents a lot of things from going wrong. On-ice nutrition is something you should consider for each outing, and I'm not talking about choosing your favorite chocolate bar from a convenience store en route to your fishing destination. There are some basic nutrition concepts to keep in mind when heading outdoors during the winter.

The first is that your body requires energy to stay warm. There's a lot to be said for starting your day off with a big, healthy breakfast. Eating right at the start of the day stokes your internal furnace and restores energy levels depleted while you slept and dreamt of catching a big one.

Don't forget that a full day on the ice with plenty of walking can give you a decent workout. I've yet to track the distance I walk on an average outing, but it's often enough exercise for me to ensure that I pack plenty of food and snack throughout the day on top of eating a decent lunch. To make things simple, I pack easy-to-eat snacks. I'm a big fan of mixed nuts,

trail mix, and granola bars. Apples and cut-up vegetables are great too. Chocolate bars and chips can be a nice treat, but don't make this your main option out there.

For lunches, I usually stick with sandwiches, although you can get pretty creative reheating foil-wrapped snacks on a portable heater. Some of my favorites are grilled cheese sandwiches and English muffins stuffed with eggs and ham. If you want to indulge yourself, pack a small portable stove and cook a hot meal. Last winter, a friend prepared venison stew in a pressure-cooker on the ice for lunch. It was a bitterly cold day and that stew was by far one of the best tasting meals I've had in the great outdoors.

In addition to eating to keep your energy reserves up, staying properly hydrated is also important. This helps your body fight off chills and stay warm. I keep it simple and bring a large bottle filled with water. I've also developed the habit of chugging a fair amount of water before I leave my vehicle for the day to go fishing. Bringing coffee in a thermos can be a great treat and a bit of a pick-me-up on the ice, but keep in mind that it's a diuretic, so drink more water accordingly. Avoid alcohol completely when ice fishing. Another diuretic, it works against your body's ability to warm itself and also impairs judgment.

Get in the habit of bringing more food than you anticipate needing. I've already mentioned a couple of times that fishing trips have a way of lasting longer than expected when the fish are biting, and extra food will come in handy. It's also a big benefit when someone forgets their lunch or doesn't pack enough. On the off-chance you get stranded somewhere (for instance, the ATV doesn't start), the extra calories will be critical to keeping warm. I usually bring about 25% more food than I think I need. I also squirrel away emergency stashes of granola bars in my jacket and bib pockets as well as my ice fishing shelter at the start of each season. Trust me, they'll be munched on over the winter.

Finally, make sure you pack out all the garbage you bring on the ice. None of us want to arrive at our favorite spot to be greeted by litter. Keep a small plastic bag in your shelter as a garbage container for your party's rubbish and other litter you spot.

Wrap Up

Keeping safety in mind when ice fishing is the best way to ensure your outings remain free of emergency situations. Exercise caution when evaluating ice conditions and pack the suggested safety gear and food to be prepared. Also consider taking a basic first aid course, as well as one in wilderness or back-country methods. I hope you'll never need to use these skills, but the training they provide will help you be prepared for a crisis should one arise.

GEAR CHECKLIST

To help you plan and pack your ice fishing outings, here's a checklist of gear outlined in the preceding chapters.

CLOTHING

Base Layer

- » Socks
- » Long underwear
- » Wicking t-shirt
- » Wicking long sleeve shirt

Middle Layer

- » Synthetic long sleeve shirt
- » Long sleeve fleece
- » Polyester and nylon, or fleece pants

Outer Layer

- » Flotation suit
- » Parka jacket
- » Pants or Bibs
- » Boots
- » Mitts or gloves
- » Hat
- » Neck warmer, balaclava

Miscellaneous

- » Sunscreen
- » Sunglasses
- » Lip balm

GEAR AND TACKLE

- » Fishing license
- » Rods - ultra-light, light, medium, medium-heavy, heavy
- » Rod case
- » Tip-ups - below water, above water
- » Tip-up lights or strike indicators
- » Tip-up depth finder and line marker
- » Extra spools of fishing line

Lures
- » Jigging spoons
- » Jigging minnows
- » Ice Jigs
- » Plastics and soft-baits

Terminal Tackle
- » Snaps, swivels, and snap-swivels
- » Hooks - octopus, treble, circle, and bait
- » Weights and sinkers - split shot, egg, and rubber core
- » Leaders
- » Floats
- » Tackle trays

Bait
- » Minnows, bucket and aerator, and bait net
- » Maggots and/or waxworms

Miscellaneous Tackle & Other Useful Gear
- » Release tools - pliers, forceps, hemostats, and scissors
- » Measuring tape (if fishing in areas with size limit regulations)
- » Headlamp, flashlight, or lantern
- » Portable propane heater
- » Backpack

AUGERS
- » Hand or power auger
- » Mixed gas and spare oil
- » Auger kit - spare blades, tools, and spark plug
- » Chisel
- » Skimmer

SHELTER
- » Shelter , sled, and/or bucket/chair
- » Cover
- » Lights
- » Inside hanger
- » Ice anchor
- » Shovel

» Extra rope
» Towing bar
» License (if applicable)

ELECTRONICS

» Sonar - flasher or LCD (case and battery)
» Battery charger (on multi-day trips)
» Underwater camera
» Hand-held GPS
» GPS spare batteries
» GPS map card (if applicable)

SAFETY GEAR

» Flotation suit or PFD
» Ice chisel
» Ice cleats
» Ice picks
» Throw rope
» Spare clothes
» First aid kit
» Survival kit
» Completed itinerary (fishing times, lake location, closest town, cell phone numbers, vehicle information) left with someone at home

FOOD AND WATER

» Snacks - trail mix, nuts, granola bars, dried fruit or cut fresh fruit and vegetables, chocolate bars, chips, jerky, cookies, etc
» Drinks - water, coffee and thermos, soda, sports drinks
» On-ice meals - sandwiches, soup or chili in thermos
» Portable stove, cookware

7

FINDING WINTER'S BEST SPORT FISH

FACTORS INFLUENCING FISH ACTIVITY
THE WINTER SEASON

Photo courtesy of Northland Fishing Tackle

FINDING WINTER'S BEST SPORT FISH

This section of the book gets into the details of how-to catch the most popular winter sport fish through the ice. For each species, I'll provide a description of where to find them during the hard-water season, and the most productive baits and presentation methods to use to catch them. These chapters also contain sidebars titled Ice Angling Essentials, which are practices and tips that are sure to improve your on-ice game. But before jumping into species specifics, I want to introduce a few important concepts that will help you understand where to find winter's best sport fish.

FACTORS INFLUENCING FISH ACTIVITY, BEHAVIOR, AND LOCATION

You can't catch fish if you can't find them and this is one of the biggest hurdles in angling, regardless of the season. How fish choose their habitat is influenced by factors like water temperature, dissolved oxygen levels, food availability, cover to hide from predators, and current, among other things. There is still more for scientists and anglers to learn about the interplay of these variables, but we do know a few things.

Water temperature impacts fish behavior and activity. In fact, it has such a big influence on fish it's sometimes referred to as the "master factor" by biologists. The icy cold waters of winter cause the activity level of many species to slow down compared to summer. Of course, every species reacts differently to water temperature. Lake trout thrive in cold water and are full of vigor beneath the ice. Walleye and northern pike are relatively active in winter too. Warm-water fish, like bluegills and bass, are not as comfortable in winter's frigid waters, but it doesn't mean that they hibernate. On the contrary, they go through blips of activity, but it pales in comparison to the bustle of cold-water fish during winter. In the following chapters, I'll highlight the water temperature preferences of different fish and the impact this has on their activity.

It's important to note that during winter there will be different layers of cold water in a lake. The majority of the water will be around 4ºC (39ºF), except for a thin colder layer directly beneath the ice. This happens because water is most dense at 4ºC, so the colder "lighter" water floats on top of the slightly warmer "denser" water below. As ice thickness increases in winter, the band of colder water directly beneath the ice deepens. This can contribute to fish leaving the frigid shallower water and moving to deeper areas where the water's less cold (i.e., 4 ºC).

Oxygen content also impacts fish location and activity. In winter, dissolved oxygen levels drop for many reasons. Increasing snow cover and ice thickness reduce light penetration. This impacts the production of oxygen by vegetation through photosynthesis. Ice cover also eliminates the infusion of oxygen into the water through wind and wave action.

Large, deep infertile (oligotrophic) lakes maintain good oxygen levels in winter because of their volume and other factors. In fertile (eutrophic) lakes, however, oxygen counts can decrease enough to impact fish locations. For instance, fish will avoid shallow areas where the decomposition of dead plants will consume and diminish levels of oxygen. Decaying organic material on the lake bottom will also use up oxygen. This results in the lowest oxygen levels being near bottom and the maximum counts being directly beneath the ice. Fish will suspend higher up in the water column as they seek out the richer oxygen levels. During a long and harsh

A cold-water species, whitefish are particularly rambunctious in winter.

Jack Levert with a late-ice bluegill.

winter, oxygen levels can drop to toxic lows on small fertile lakes, resulting in winterkill, the massive die-off of fish.

Food is another significant factor influencing fish location. I discuss this in detail for different species in the following chapters, but it's worth noting here. Winter's a hardship period for many species and fish will gravitate to areas with a good food supply. The abundance and proximity of forage that requires little energy to capture is very important to a fish surviving the frozen-water period. Winter food ranges from minnows to microscopic edibles, like zooplankton.

Structures and cover that allow fish to hide from predators or ambush prey are other important ingredients in the locations that fish choose to inhabit. As an example, sunfish will relate to weeds or wood for food but also for protection from larger predators, like pike. Fish must choose their habitat for opportunities to eat but also to seek cover and hide from predators to lessen the chances of becoming a meal themselves.

Current will also influence fish location. Back bays and side channels in rivers are common overwintering areas for many species, as fish will avoid the main channel's fast flow in order to conserve energy. In lakes, current's important as it brings oxygen and food with it. This is why feeder streams often attract fish. Remember: always be cautious around current as it reduces ice thickness and safety.

The above are just a few of the many intertwined elements influencing fish location and behavior. There is still much to learn about the interplay of these factors as well as others, such as the influence of photoperiod (the recurring cycle of light and dark periods), for example. What's important is being aware of these factors as you analyze the outcomes of your ice fishing outings in different lake and river environments. This will improve your understanding of the activity levels and location preferences of different fish species beneath the ice.

THE WINTER SEASON

I want to introduce a timeline for the ice fishing season. In areas with consistent ice cover for several months, the winter season can be divided into three periods: early, mid, and late winter. These phases give us a framework to approach ice fishing and talk about things like fish locations and their activity levels.

Early Winter and First Ice

The early winter period begins with the first day of safe ice. The ice season starts initially on small bodies of water like ponds, pits, and back bays before larger lakes and rivers freeze over. This period lasts only a few weeks, but first ice delivers great fishing action. This is mainly due to fish continuing their autumn eating binge to stock up energy reserves for the harsh winter ahead. The arrival of a few inches of ice overhead changes little for fish in the short term. As snow accumulates on ice and consistently cold temperatures continue we enter the midwinter phase.

Midwinter

The midwinter phase can be a challenging time to be an ice angler. The hedonistic gorging's over and many fish slip into a state of torpor as cold water temperatures cause a reduction in metabolism and activity levels. In terms of general ice fishing trends, midwinter is often a time when many fish, if they didn't already do so in autumn, move to deeper areas like humps or mid-basin flats. Overall fishing can be tough. Success is often based on finesse presentations, focusing on productive water (such as large, deep lakes instead of shallow, small ones), and fishing periods of peak activity (e.g., twilight for walleye).

Late Winter

The late winter phase represents a resurgence of ice fishing action. There are no rules for when this period starts, but fishing gets better closer to season's end. The increasing intensity and duration of daylight triggers an instinctual switch in fish that alerts them to spring's approach. Feeding kicks into high-gear to replenish their depleted energy reserves. Warm, melt water slips beneath the ice near shore ushering in oxygen and nutrients, giving the shallows a boost of important food-chain ingredients. Several species will stage in or near shallow spawning areas during this phase. Increasing sunlight also stimulates plant activity from tiny phytoplankton to larger vegetation. Late ice is when you see green weeds beneath your ice hole or bring up plant pieces after drilling holes in shallow water.

The Winter Dance

We start out the season in closer to shore, it could be shallow or deep water. As we get into midwinter in January or February, the shallower areas' water gets colder than 39 degrees [Fahrenheit] and some of the bays actually get short on oxygen and fish move out into the lake. So we ... fish deeper water and mid-lake spots, like humps and points that extend out into the lake. Then as March comes and the sun gets higher in the sky, the snow starts to melt and the water starts to run, the bays get re-oxygenated and brought back to life and the fish move into the bays.

Dave Genz, Modern Ice Fishing Pioneer and Expert, MN

The late season is one of the best times to fish, but as ice thickness recedes and freeze-thaw cycles begin, safety becomes an increasingly critical issue as ice becomes progressively less predictable.

With these basics outlined we're ready to dive into an overview of a variety of sport fish worthy of pursuit through the ice, beginning with one of the most popular game fish in North America - walleye.

WALLEYE

Jeff "Gussy" Gustafson with a walleye taken at sunset.

Small yellow perch rank high on a walleye's diet.

WALLEYE

Few fish conjure the twinkle of excitement in an ice angler's eyes as much as walleye. Extremely sought-after throughout the year, these predators are pursued for both the challenge of the sport as well as their delectable taste on the dinner table. In this chapter, I'll help you understand walleye winter behavior, common locations, and the top baits and fishing tactics to catch them. This section also lays the ground work for several important ice fishing concepts, like the mechanics of jigging for example.

SPECIES SUMMARY

Walleye are classified as a cool-water species. They flourish in a range of lake and river environments, remaining fairly active during the winter. Color-wise, walleye are dark on top, and their sides range from olive-green to gold, depending on water clarity and their environment. Walleye have a white tip on their lower tail and it's often the give-away feature to anglers spotting the shape of their catch down the ice hole. Another distinguishing trait of walleye are their silvery eyes. The foggy eyeball lets walleye see extremely well in low-light conditions, a characteristic that gives them an advantage over the majority of their prey. For this reason, day-to-night transitions are prime times to fish walleye. Voracious hunters, these fish aren't picky. They'll eat morsels in a range of sizes depending on availability, but walleye have a particular affinity for yellow perch, and the two populations are seldom far from each other.

FINDING WALLEYE BENEATH THE ICE

It's important to consider what phase of the winter you're in when looking for walleye beneath the ice. During the initial weeks of the ice season, targeting walleye where you found them late in the fall is always a good start. Come late autumn, these fish migrate toward winter holding areas, such as deep water points and humps (see below).

In some instances on fertile lakes you may find them outside of bays holding healthy vegetation. Green weeds will attract and hold baitfish and walleye won't be far behind. These zones can be particularly productive during twilight. Once you find good greenery, try to position yourself on weed lines near breaks, like those found on drop-offs or growing on points. Predators and edges go hand-in-hand, so learn to find these key areas and you'll hook more fish.

Once midwinter arrives, walleye often move to deeper water as weeds die off in the shallows. This is the time to target features like off shore humps and points. In some instances fish may have already moved to these deeper water structures in autumn. Don't forget to factor in their food source, such as perch schools, when trying to locate midwinter walleye.

As the end of winter approaches, walleye activity can really heat up. It's worth nothing that in many provinces and states, the walleye season usually ends before late winter, but in regions where the season remains open the action's great the last few weeks of remaining ice. Walleye spawn shortly after ice break-up and move toward spawning areas before the ice recedes. On lakes, expect them to hold around inflows and outflows such as creeks or streams, outside of bays, or near rocky shoal spawning sites.

On rivers, deep back bays and side channels will hold walleye all winter, but first ice action is often fantastic. Deep holes are daytime holding zones in rivers, while shallow flats on inside bends, current seams,

Dusk is a prime time to fish walleye.

Finding walleye in midwinter often means jigging deeper structures.

and points serve as low-light hunting grounds. At late ice on rivers look for fish to stage near tributaries in deep pools or slack water spots.

Top Structures

When looking for walleye, key structures to focus on are humps, points, and saddles. Proximity to deep water will boost the potential of these spots. Let's look at these areas in a bit more detail.

A point is a piece of structure that juts out into deep water off of shore or an island. They range in shapes and sizes but ultimately points extend into and are surrounded by deeper water. The variation in depth that they provide, combined with fast access to deep water make points attractive to most fish, walleye included. These structures get a lot of attention from anglers as they're relatively easy to spot by following the extension of a shoreline point into the water. When choosing points consider that the larger the structure the more fish it's likely to hold.

One of my favorite spots on a large, deep lake is an underwater point that extends for roughly 150 yards. The middle to end of the point drops from 15 to 35 feet of water. At dawn and dusk we concentrate our jigging efforts on the shallower zone between 15 and 25 feet of water on the top of the point. During the day we'll slip into the deeper 30-plus feet when fish are inactive. Sometimes we'll experience mid-day bouts of activity, when walleye will aggressively chase schools of perch up onto the point. For this reason, we regularly drill plenty of holes over the top, sides, and deep edges of this structure to be prepared to quickly hole hop to try and intercept these cruising fish.

The same fish-attraction structural qualities of points also make humps a common winter-walleye residence, especially at midwinter. A hump is an uprising in the bottom depth. They're also referred to as bars, reefs, or sunken islands. Fishing guide, Jeff Gustafson of Kenora, Ontario, is a big fan of fishing humps for walleye.

"The absolute key area to spend your time fishing on nearly any hump is a flat area in the prime depth zone of the lake you're fishing. Using Lake of the Woods as an example, walleye show up mostly in the 25-30 foot zone. So that being said, humps, no matter where they top off, that have significant flats in the 25-30 foot zone are hot. If you drill on a hump and find flats in the 15 foot zone, they are likely not as good, because the prime spot is too shallow. There are exceptions of course, like edges (drop-offs, sand/rock, or weed/sand) but for the most part, flats on structure are the best walleye locations you will find," he says.

What do you get when you combine two humps with points? A saddle. This structure is best described as follows. Picture you're holding a rubber band in two hands, so it's straight. Move your hands together and the band drops - there's your saddle. Your thumbs and forefingers represent either humps or islands, which could vary in size and shape, and the bends in the band are the sloping, connected ridges that join these two land masses. Sometimes these slopes are relatively uniform, as in the rubber band example, while in other instances one side may extend farther or drop faster than the other.

Points, humps, and saddles serve as the basis for a lot of walleye ice fishing. Walleye can be found anywhere on these three structures, so it's important to be thorough. Daytime holding zones are often the deeper breaks or edges of the structures. Look for walleye to hold at the base of a break where a steep slope ends and meets a uniform basin flat. The top portion of these structures are often reserved for low-light hunting. Walleye will move up from deeper, holding areas to invade the shallows to ambush perch and baitfish.

From here, it's individual details that make certain areas of these structures more appealing than others. For example, if one side of a point is more like a wall that quickly drops in depth, while the other side holds a gentle slope, expect walleye to hold on the more gradual slope. It's simply

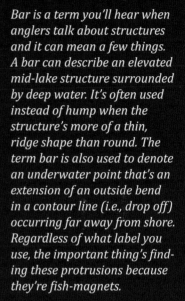

Setting the Bar High

Bar is a term you'll hear when anglers talk about structures and it can mean a few things. A bar can describe an elevated mid-lake structure surrounded by deep water. It's often used instead of hump when the structure's more of a thin, ridge shape than round. The term bar is also used to denote an underwater point that's an extension of an outside bend in a contour line (i.e., drop off) occurring far away from shore. Regardless of what label you use, the important thing's finding these protrusions because they're fish-magnets.

Davis Viehbeck uses his sonar to check depth as Dave Bennett looks on. The two anglers are trying to pinpoint a drop off during a search for daytime walleye.

Structure Snow Tracks

Using snow machine or ATV tracks is a great trick to create a visual reference of the structure beneath you. Ice angler Dustin "Dusty" Minke of Forest Lake, MN explains the process as follows. With a GPS displaying the lake contours in hand, drive around the structure to create an outline with your tracks. Now everyone in your fishing party can see the size and shape of the area you're fishing. Once you start drilling and checking holes with a portable sonar, write the depth in the snow beside each one. Now you've got depth reference points to supplement your vehicle mapping tracks, such as where it's shallow and where it's deep. Comparing nearby holes also gives you an idea of how steep the slopes are on the different sides. This track-mapping trick works particularly well for large structures, like mid-lake humps and long points.

"Sometimes this doesn't work because there's no snow, so we have one guy carry the GPS and the flasher along with the scoop. His job is to check depth, scoop holes and navigate the designated driller to where to cut the next hole, kind of like a pilot and a co pilot," Minke says.

an easier route for them to make deep to shallow water movements. If you're fishing a river or reservoir with current, expect fish to hold on the downstream side or tip of the point in slack water waiting to ambush prey.

Small fingers, which could be described as miniature points, and inside bends on the above three structures also have a tendency to funnel fish movements. Rock piles and weed edges are also attractive to walleye. Essentially, once you locate a large structure holding walleye, the trick becomes fine-tuning your position to look for additional features that will concentrate fish. These zones are often called "the spot on the spot" and represent prime real estate for fish. When looking for Mr. Silver Eyes, paying attention to these subtle nuances will catch you more fish.

JIGGING TACTICS FOR WALLEYE

Look through the tackle boxes of a serious walleye ice angler and you'll likely see an assortment of lures including spoons, jigging minnows, and jigs. They'll probably have a selection of confidence baits they've used to

Dustin "Dusty" Minke with a jigged-up walleye.
Photo: Jeff Gustafson

catch dozens of walleye in the past, from wide-wobbling spoons to small, ice jigs. Wise walleye anglers know being prepared for any mood a fish may be in betters your odds.

Jigging Spoons

Walleye jigging spoons come in an array of shapes and sizes. Beyond weight, the best way to categorize spoons is according to the action they deliver in the water.

The most rambunctious dancers are bent models. The degree of intensity of a spoon's action and flash is often determined by its bend and width, since these factors increase water resistance. The lures deliver an erratic sway when lifted and wobble when dropped. Examples include the Northland Fire-Eye Minnow, Custom Jigs Spins Slender Spoon, Acme

As dusk approaches, Rob Jackson watches his sonar for fish signals after finishing a lift-fall jigging sequence.

ICE ANGLING ESSENTIALS ⟫

BASIC JIGGING MOVES - TRANSLATING INTEREST INTO BITES:

Jigging is a two-part game. Baits must not only get a fish's interest but also seduce them to bite. Aggressive fish often don't need much persuading, but neutral or inactive ones usually will require finessing. In the vertical jigging approach of ice fishing, the attraction of a jigging move is accomplished by the lift-fall of the bait. Whether you're using a spoon, ice jig, jigging minnow, or another style of lure, the lift-fall element of jigging is what creates movement, vibrations, and flash to get the attention of nearby fish. Depending on the action you're after, you can lift the lure anywhere from a few inches to over a foot. Now, if you continuously lift and drop a jig without pause you might get the odd aggressive fish, but your presentation becomes deadlier when you mix in pauses as well as smaller hops and micro shakes. Now you're faking something tasty! In the same way stopping a crankbait during a retrieve in open water triggers hits, so does pausing and holding a jigging lure still beneath the ice. After all, you need to give fish the opportunity to hit your offering. Pauses may range from a couple-to-30 seconds or more depending on the mood of the fish.

So, the fundamental elements to any jigging recipe include: raises, drops, shakes, and pauses. With these basic ingredients down, you can add your own special flavor to your offering by experimenting with things like how aggressively you snap or lift the bait, whether you let it freefall or drop it on a controlled line, the number of lifts and drops before a pause, and the amount of time you pause a bait and so on.

A jigging spoon is one of the most productive lures to catch walleye beneath the ice.

The Northland Macho Minnow's a deadly spoon for walleye.

Phoebe, Williams Wabler or Whitefish, Lindy Original Viking Spoon, JB Lures Angle Eye, and Blue Fox Rattle Flash Jig'n Spoon and More-silda.

The wild action of bent spoons attracts fish from a distance and riles-up aggressive ones to strike. These baits do well when fish are active. These types of spoons call in fish. Walleye might not always hit them, but these baits will often pique their curiosity and draw them in close enough that you can spot them on your electronics. Fish these lures with a quick lift of the arm or a snap of the wrist. Then let them freefall on slack or semi-taught line so as not to inhibit their tantalizing action. Add in a pause for several seconds before jigging the bait again, and be sure to mix in some subtle shakes of the rod after the pause, as this often entices strikes.

Gliders are another type of jigging spoon, like the Bay de Noc Vingla or the Lindy Techni-Glo Rattl'n Flyer Spoon. These lures have small wings on their sides that cause them to glide outward as they fall. These spoons let you cover a larger area under the ice. Their gliding action is also great to call in fish from a distance.

These lures work well on a medium-paced lift combined with a freefall on slack line. On the fall, the lure will glide out to the side. Once the spoon's weight pulls the line taut it sways back to the center until the line hangs straight. This is a feature to keep in mind, as you will need to include a long enough pause to allow the spoon to swing back into place. Hold it still for a few seconds or jiggle it to trigger a hit before jigging again. This isn't to say that quick snaps of the wrist followed by a long pause won't call in fish and catch them, just be careful not to overwork glider-style baits.

As you might expect, the final category of spoons contrasts the bent options and are simply called straight spoons. Keep in mind here, that although they're straight, they're not flat. Spoons need curves and contours to sway in the water. These lures deliver a toned-down action, a tighter wobble, and less flash. A variety of these options are available on the market; proven producers include the Northland Macho Minnow and Buck-Shot Rattle Spoon, Lindy Frostee Jigging Spoon, Bay de Noc Swedish Pimple, Hopkins Smoothie, JB Lures Varmit, Luhr-Jensen Crippled Herring or Cast Champ, and Acme Kastmaster.

Straight spoons serve many purposes. One advantage is that they drop faster than wide-wobbling spoons. This is handy when fishing deeper water or when time is limited. Over the course of a 45-minute dusk bite, having a spoon that quickly sinks to the bottom may catch you more fish. The other benefit to these baits is that their more conservative action often appeals to neutral or negative mood fish, as well as aggressive ones. They are often the better option when faced with the typical tough fishing conditions of mid-day, midwinter, or cold fronts, which are notorious for dampening fish activity. Fish these spoons on the standard raise-fall-pause pattern, but experiment with it. For example, don't be afraid to add two small snaps to the lift before letting the bait fall downward.

Straight spoons can also be used for dropper rigs. A spoon dropper is a finesse presentation where the bottom hook is removed and a short dropper line of a few inches is tied on. Commercial droppers are also available. The other end of the dropper holds the baited hook. The flash of the spoon attracts fish and the morsel of a small, baited hook is often too much for walleye to resist. I'll discuss dropper rigs in more detail in the yellow perch, crappie, and sunfish chapters.

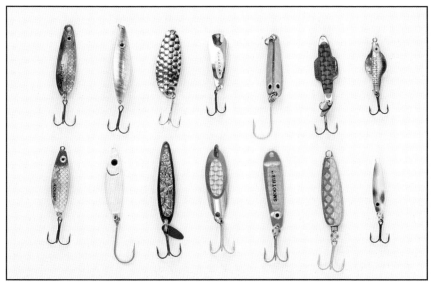

A sampling of walleye jigging spoons. The top row are bent models (L-R) Northland Fire-Eye Minnow, Blue Fox Flash Spoon, ACME Tackle Company Little Cleo, Custom Jigs and Spins Slender Spoon, HT Enterprises Jig-A-Whopper Hawger Spoon; the last two spoons, the Bay-de-Noc Vingla and the Lindy Rattl'n Flyer Spoon, are gliders. The bottom row holds several straight spoons including: the Northland Buck-Shot Rattle Spoon, Luhr Jensen Crippled Herring, Bay-de-Noc Swedish Pimple, Luhr Jensen Cast Champ, Hopkins Smoothie, Bass'n Bait Company Rattle Snakie, JB Lures Rattling Varmit.

Don Theoret with a nice walleye.

Jigging Minnows

Jigging minnows, also called swimming lures, are another popular style of lures for walleye. The Northland Puppet Minnow, Rapala Jigging Shad Rap, Nils Master Hali Aatu, and Force Lures Quick Strike Minnow are some examples. Jigging minnows have a natural, horizontal fish profile and, on certain days, walleye prefer this positioning over vertically shaped spoons. The tail of these baits have fins, causing the lure to swim in an arc when dropped. The centre line tie on the lure also encourages the bait to jiggle slightly in response to subtle shakes.

The basic jigging sequence consists of a raise-fall-pause pattern. Lifts should be around a foot or so. Then let the bait freefall and give the lure plenty of time to fly outwards and then sweep back to the center of the hole. This lazy circling decent is a close replica of a dying minnow. Once at center, pause the bait for a while before starting the next move, and there are a few options to choose from.

One of the best anglers I've seen work a jigging minnow is Lake of the Woods guide, Dave Bennett, who's a fan of "pumping" these lures. The action serves as a middle ground between the sequence described above and extremely subtle jiggles. He often pumps the bait once he marks a fish on his sonar. Pumping consists of a series of 3 to 5 lift-drops that move the bait roughly 4 to 5 inches. He uses controlled drops on taught line to keep a feel for the bait at all times. In this situation the goal isn't to cause the bait to glide, but rather to use its profile and a tight-action to attract fish.

If you attract a fish with either a lift-fall or pumping action, hold the bait still before trying more subtle triggering moves. Light shakes cause the bait to rock back and forth or roll side to side. One of Bennett's best moves to evoke hits from on-looking fish is an extremely slight down-tap of the rod tip. "The tap's enough to get the bottom treble to dance under the bait. This treble-hook shake often triggers fish to bite," he says. Worth noting though is that Bennett modifies his jigging minnows. He adds a split ring to the centre treble hook to encourage this tantalizing swinging action. If unsuccessful with his down tap maneuver, Bennett suggests raising the bait up a few inches from the fish. This move often either forces the fish to commit and chase or let a meal escape. He'll try raising the bait several times. If unsuccessful with these finesse moves but he still is marking fish on his electronics, he'll start all over again with a big lift-fall jigging sequence and tweak his presentation slightly until he cracks the code and gets a bite.

Other Jigging Baits

I want to touch on two other styles of walleye jigging baits. Darters baits, like the Salmo Chubby Darter and the Lindy Darter, feature realistic paint patterns and a minnow profile that make them a great walleye jigging option. These lures work well on a standard lift-fall-hold pattern. On the lift, the bait swims upwards with a tight, wobbling action, and falls with a seductive shimmy. Shakes, small hops, and tiny jerks all add realism to the offering. As a tip, fishing it with a snap will give the lure room to wiggle whereas tying direct can limit this action.

Blade baits are another walleye jigging lure. Examples of these lures include the Reef Runner Cicada or Heddon Sonar. With a thin profile, blade baits put out a lot of flash and vibrations, making them excellent search lures. Experiment with both quick snaps of the wrist and slower raises, as at times fish may prefer one speed to the other.

Baiting Up Spoons and Jigging Minnows

Most walleye anglers tip lures with bait, and minnows are the most popular when it comes to walleye. Popular walleye minnows include shiners, dace, chubs, and suckers. What is critical when tipping is to ensure that the added bait doesn't interfere with the lure's action. If you're new to ice angling, jig spoons and other lures a few feet down the hole at first while

A walleye fooled by a Salmo Chubby Darter.

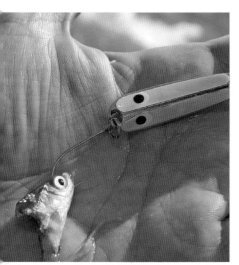

Pictured here is the minnow-head tipping technique on a Jig-A-Whopper Hawger Spoon.

The three-minnow hooking technique works when trophy-hunting walleye.

watching them to ensure all is well with your offering.

Jigging minnows are best rigged with a minnow head on the center treble hook to keep the lure balanced. One method is tipping the head or the tail-facing point of the treble. Some trophy anglers will also gob on several heads to each point of the treble. You can also tip the front and rear single hooks on jigging minnows with minnow heads or tail meat as well. Remember to add fresh bait every 20 minutes or so to keep the scent trail flowing.

Treble hooks on spoons offer choices for bait-rigging. For smaller sized spoons or to simply add some scent, tip one hook with a minnow head or tail. Of course there's nothing wrong with tipping a spoon with an entire minnow as well. When trophy hunting big walleye, many anglers use small 1.5- to 2-inch minnows, tipping each point of the treble hook with bait. This presentation is definitely more of a meal than a snack.

Except for trophy hunting or when walleye are aggressive, I'm a fan of using a minnow head. The hooked minnow head serves as a bull's-eye; fish seldom bite short with this rigging as they might when using a full minnow. When using minnow heads, I find the following is best, although it's a tad graphic to describe: Pinch the head off of a minnow below where the spine meets the skull. As you pull the head away from the body, leave some of the guts attached. The entrails boost the scent of the offering and also add an alluring effect when you gently shake a spoon. Delicious.

Several winters ago, the effectiveness of entrails hit home while I was team fishing with several anglers for daytime walleye. Some of our party were having better success than others. Walleye weren't aggressive and would only hit subtly jigged spoons. When the unsuccessful anglers in our fishing party asked for help, we loaned them some of our spoons that were catching fish and suggested they use the head and entrails tipping technique. After this our pals quickly joined in the action.

Anglers should also embrace artificial tipping options when it comes to spoons and jigging minnows. I'll often cut off the forked tail of a Berkley Gulp! Minnow adding it to a treble hook on spoons. A whole minnow can also be used. Berkley also makes a Minnow Head for tipping spoons and jigging minnows as well. Other options include tipping baits with finesse plastics to add a teasing action to the business end of baits.

Ice Jigs

As I noted earlier, ice jigs are simply weighted hooks ranging in horizontal to vertical orientations in the water. There are dozens of standard lead head jigs on the market, in a range of weights. Many of them are perfect for tipping with a lively minnow or soft bait artificial and jigging for walleye.

When it comes to jigging, a good rule of thumb is to use the lightest jig possible. You need enough weight to get to bottom and be able to feel your bait. Use too much and a walleye might sense the unnatural weight and either not fully take the offering or spit it out before you can set the hook. Jigs between 1/8- to 3/8-ounces will serve you well for most walleye situations.

Horizontal ice jigs get the call when I'm using whole minnows in a steady jigging repertoire. The majority of the time, I use a ball head horizontal jig when rigging with a minnow. These baits lift and fall on a fairly straight line. To get a gliding arc out of your jigs, use a glider-style jig head like a Lindy Techni-Glo Flyer. This jig head has small wings on its side, giving the bait a gliding circular fall; work it as you would a glider spoon. Another variation is using a propeller bladed jig, like the Northland Whistler Jig, that helicopters on a slow fall while sending out vibrations to trigger bites.

One way to tip horizontal jigs with minnows is to rig the bait through the head, coming up from the bottom jaw and out the skull. This often kills the minnow, but steady jigging moves keep the bait looking lively. Another option is using a long-shank jig hook, and hooking the minnow through the lower lip, out the gill plate, and then through the back. This rigging saves bait when snapping jigs. If I'm aiming for a finesse approach, I'll opt for a lighter hooking method, coming out through the nostril or lips so as not to kill the bait. The downside to this light rigging is that if you get aggressive with your jigging sequence, the bait will often rip off. Another potential problem, however, is that light-biting walleye could be able to steal your minnow without getting hooked. One option to combat light-biting fish is to use the rigging I first described – through the jaw and out the skull. Unfortunately, sometimes walleye will only hit a minnow if it's alive, in which case, using a stinger hook might land you more fish than a plain jig and minnow combination.

Vertical ice jigs also have a role in walleye angling. When lazy lifts and slow controlled drops are the ticket to tempting shy walleye to bite, I find that vertical jigs such as the Northland Forage Minnow Jig, Lindy

> ### Bait Bucket Dumping »
>
> *Never release live bait or dump the contents of a bait bucket into any waters (i.e., down an ice hole). In most areas, this practice is illegal as it can introduce non-native species into a water system. Whenever possible, save leftover bait and freeze it to be used another day. Also use live bait from the waters you intend to fish instead of transporting bait in from other areas. This helps prevent the spread of invasive species and viruses like viral hemorrhagic septicemia (VHS).*

Frostee, and JB Lures Big Max do well for this presentation.

My favorite way to present minnows using vertical jigs is to hook them behind the dorsal fin. The hook faces forward, so when a walleye takes the minnow, it's positioned perfectly for the hook set. It's critical to hook the minnow on either side of its spine. Touch the minnow's backbone with the hook and you'll likely paralyze it (and it's the lively ones that attract walleye). Done properly, this hooking method is a great way to anchor a struggling minnow close to or right on the lake's bottom. The minnow will give the presentation action by continuously struggling to right itself but you should also mix in some light hops or slow controlled lifts and falls to get a walleye's attention. Banging these baits on bottom and then resting them on the floor will also call in fish. This low-key approach has iced me plenty of walleye when more aggressive jigging options weren't producing results.

A back-hooked minnow dropped to the bottom makes a great presentation as the baitfish struggles to right itself.

ICE ANGLING ESSENTIALS »»

MORE JIGGING TIPS

By now, I'm sure you're beginning to appreciate the nuances of jigging and how much room there is for experimentation. I'd like to offer more tips that will serve you well for walleye, and for other species too.

Be careful not to overwork baits. I've seen anglers get excited as the setting sun casts a warm glow over a frozen lake, signaling the start of the walleye night bite. Overly anxious, they conduct their jigging rods with gusto as if they've had too much coffee. In most cases, a rule to follow is "if you think you're working your lures slowly enough, slow down a little more." This doesn't mean that you need to barely lift the jig or do so extremely slowly. On the contrary, you still want to jig the bait—but it's the pauses and regular subtle quivers to the rod that will trigger fish to hit. Remember to watch your sonar for fish signals, tweaking your presentation to match their interest and activity level. Once you start catching fish, experiment by speeding things up a little bit. When fish are aggressive, you can sometimes catch them by jigging quickly, but for the most part, if you're marking fish on your electronics and can't get them to bite, slowing down is often the ticket.

Another tip is when walleye aren't aggressive avoid quickly dropping a bait right in their faces. This can spook inactive fish, so it's best to work a lure slowly down to a foot above marked fish when using big lift-drop sequences.

In Chapter 5, I spoke about the learning opportunities underwater cameras provide. When it comes to jigging lures, cameras can help you understand the action and finer points of the lure you're using. For instance, watching a jigging minnow, you'll see how long you need to pause to let the lure swing back to center. With a bent spoon, you may find that by adding a small twitch during its fall, you can add a subtle kick to the lure that sends off a vibrant flash. Setting your bait at rest and then watching it as you hop or quiver it lets you see how these rod movements add a nervous jiggling to the lure, and helps you to see which gestures catch you fish. Observing these finesse moves with the camera will also likely teach you that a less-is-more approach to jigging is often most effective in triggering hits. It will also show you the way these lure quivers can make the minnow meat you've added move teasingly.

Another jigging tip I want to touch on is the importance of returning lures to their original starting position at the end of each drop. Let me explain. Let's say you're using a straight spoon in 20 feet of water. You've positioned the spoon a foot off bottom and you're holding the rod pointing slightly downward, on a 45-degree angle. You jig the lure upwards, stopping at around 90 degrees (or straight out in front of you), which raises the lure roughly 12 inches. At this point, what's important is that you return the rod to the 45-degree position so the lure drops back to rest in 19 feet of water. Most of the time, fish hit once it comes to rest or is jiggled before you plan to jig it again. By returning the bait to the same position it was last time, you're placing it in the strike zone of inquisitive fish that swam in for a closer look. If you stop a lure each time at different depths, any fish that has come in to inspect the bait is too busy swimming up and down to track the whereabouts of the lure. You're making it difficult for them to hit it. You might get lucky if the fish is aggressive, but an inactive one will likely quickly grow disinterested and swim away. Returning the bait to the same depth simply betters the odds that fish will hit it.

Does this mean that you can't raise a lure? Not at all——and experimenting with different depths in the water column can catch you more fish. To do this, what I recommend is after pausing a bait, slowly raise the lure up to the depth you want to fish. This slow, upward and natural swimming can sometimes trigger a hit, but it also gives curious fish a chance to follow the bait upwards.

If you're fishing with a sonar, raising baits is also a great move to activate a walleye (and other fish) to strike. In essence, what you're doing is playing a game of keep-away with a walleye interested in your bait. When I'm using my flasher, I carefully watch the signal of my lure. As soon as I see a walleye, I continue jigging until its signal gets closer. Just before the walleye's signal reaches the bait, I start slowly raising my arm while jigging the lure to keep it looking lively. The goal is to raise the bait just fast enough to keep it away from the fish. Sometimes you'll get fish chasing several feet off bottom, then suddenly you hit the tipping point and they attack. In other instances, the fish may lose interest and drop towards bottom. When this happens, try and follow the signal while jigging your bait to engage their interest again. If they follow a second time, attempt a different raise-and-trigger sequence. For example, perhaps jig the bait in place for a few seconds to let the fish look at it before slowly raising it, or if the fish moves in faster, raise the bait quicker. There are no magic recipes and you'll need to fine-tune your presentation accordingly each day, but with enough time on the water you'll develop some dynamite moves to hypnotize fish to hit.

Lastly, ice fishing guide Jeff Gustafson of Kenora, Ontario offers this piece of jigging advice. "If you get walleye that are showing up on your electronics but will not bite, even if you have changed up your bait a few times, try fishing your bait higher up off bottom than you normally would, like 3-6 feet. If the water is fairly clear, walleye will see your bait. Sometimes making them commit a bit by coming up to your bait will make them more likely to strike," he says.

Steve Barnett returns his rod tip low to the ice after jigging a spoon. This gives him plenty of area to raise the rod tip when trying to charm a walleye to bite.

Downsizing Baits Can Finesse Bites During the Day

Walleye can be finicky eaters and when they're inactive they'll snub lures with a stubbornness that will make you go bananas. It's maddening when you clearly spot them on your sonar, but they just won't bite. When this happens, one option to try is downsizing (i.e., using smaller-than-average lures) and keeping presentations subtle. Whether you're fishing a clear lake or a stained river, learning to finesse walleye will make you a better angler.

Daytime fishing often calls for a finesse approach. Walleye patiently wait to hunt in their low light feeding zones at dusk, but can be tempted into biting small, finesse baits dangled in front of their noses at other times. Locating their day holding areas lets you target walleye outside of the prime time periods. Since the fish are often inactive, success usually results from subtly maneuvering small baits near bottom and drilling plenty of holes to boost your odds of putting your jig in front of a fish uninterested in moving far for a snack.

Downsizing begins by switching to lighter tackle, which often means lowering to 4-pound test line. Lure options include small 1/8-ounce spoons or 1/16-ounce ice jigs tipped with maggots, waxworms, artificial bait, or finesse plastics. I'll describe plenty of these styles of lures and tipping options in the following chapters on perch and crappie, but it's worth noting that sometimes you need these smaller presentations with walleye too.

Walleye Jigging Sticks

Medium-light to medium powered rods with extra-fast to fast action work well for most walleye jigging. The average range for walleye rods is often between 28- to 36-inches, although many 24- and 26-inch rods are available. Consider using longer rods when possible as they help facilitate strong, sweeping hook sets and provide adequate leverage during the battle. Outfit the rod with a quality reel and spool it with 6- to 10-pound-test nylon or fluorocarbon or 8- to 12-pound test superline.

The author with a walleye.

SETLINE TACTICS

Although jigging lures is a productive way to fool walleye, using setlines can also be effective. The two main methods for setlining are using dead-stick rod set-ups or tip-ups. When walleye are sluggish and not actively feeding, dead-sticking minnows often fools a couple more fish into biting. Thorne Bros. makes an incredible stick for this application. Their noodle tips signal bites before a fish feels resistance, but they have plenty of backbone to play a big walleye. On tough, midwinter bites, this do-nothing approach can sometimes out-produce subtle jigging. The technique is simple: set up a live or dead minnow on a jig or hook and weight combination and position it anywhere from 3- to 12-inches off bottom. Then it's a waiting game. Every so often, lift and slowly lower the offering. Also ensure that you keep the hole clear of ice and frequently rebait with a fresh minnow to keep it smelling tasty.

When legal to use multiple lines, I most often place my dead-stick rod a few feet from my jigging hole, either in a rod holder or on a pail. Some anglers also make a wooden 'T' to balance their rods. I like to keep my dead-stick rod close so I can get to it quickly when I have a hit. It's

⟫ Dead-sticking

The logic behind dead-sticking is that the soft tip of the rod allows a fish to pick up your bait without detecting the rod. The tip also acts as a great visual strike indicator and can also help anglers predict a looming bite from nearby fish. The soft tips of dead-stick rods really let anglers know when their bait is getting nervous often indicating a predatory fish is nearby and coming in for a closer look.

Davis Viehbeck, Ice Angler and Outdoor Writer, ON

common to attract walleye with the flash of a spoon, only to have them ignore the lure but take the nearby minnow. I like using a dead-stick over a tip-up for this application as a rod makes it easy to quickly set the hook. This is especially effective with light-biting walleye. Just remember to loosen the drag on your reel so an aggressive fish doesn't pull your rod down the hole.

For the most part, tip-ups are best used when you're targeting walleye in an area with a well-established history of holding fish. Although it doesn't take long to set tip-ups, they can sometimes foster a stay-put attitude in anglers. For this reason, I rarely put out a tip-up when I'm searching for fish. Yet if I'm going to set up on a proven shoal or a point known to produce fish at dusk, tip-ups let you increase the chances of catching a few fish in this critical feeding window. Dead-stick rods can also be used in this manner as well, just be sure you can see them well enough, as light fades, to spot a strike.

A common setline strategy is to arrive well before twilight, drilling plenty of holes to cover a variety of depths. Depending on the number of anglers in the fishing party, start by placing setlines in deep and shallow water on the periphery of the fishing area. If you have enough legal lines, begin to fill in the sides and edges of a piece of structure, like a point. These setlines are a great way to signal when the evening bite begins and the direction walleye are travelling into the area. Frequently, deep lines are often the first to go off as walleye begin to invade the shallow water to feed. Similarly, place setlines in the shallows to signal when fish have made their way to this zone.

I recall an outing with my father and four others several years ago near North Bay, Ontario. It was midwinter and we were stationed on a mid-lake hump that topped out around 20 feet. We had setlines positioned all over the structure and it was merely a matter of waiting for the fish to arrive. As the setting sun touched the tree tops the action started and it was fast. The deep setlines quickly sprung to life signaling the walleye invasion. The next 25 minutes was a flurry of activity. We were all busy helping land fish, re-setting lines, or tweaking our positioning progressively shallower as the bite wore on. Eventually the action faded and we packed it in to seek refuge by the hearth of the fireplace in our friend's nearby cottage.

In a nutshell, tip-ups and dead-stick rods can help you pinpoint where walleye are feeding, so you can close in on fish with jigging lines. With stationary lines set, hole-hop and jig for fish while monitoring setlines for a strike.

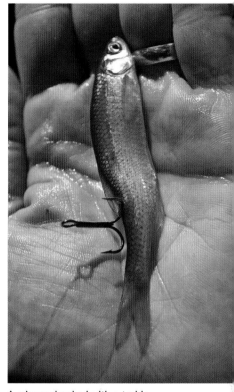

A minnow hooked with a treble for a setline.

Minnows are the best bait to use for walleye setline applications. I've experimented with different rigging combinations over the years, but usually follow the light-hooking tactics I noted above for ice jigs. Sometimes a horizontal jig is best, while on other days, walleye will be drawn in by a vertical jig. Experiment with your fishing buddies until you figure out what jig and hooking method is most effective that day. An alternative to using jigs is to place split shots a few inches above a minnow rigged on a circle, treble, or octopus hook.

To make quick work of setting tip-ups, I often use my sonar unit to watch the depth of the minnow as I lower line down the hole. If you don't have a sonar, a clip-on depth finder can be used to determine bottom. Line markers are handy to use as well, so that you can quickly reset the tip-up to the same depth after hooking and playing a fish. When using tip-ups at dusk and into the night, consider outfitting flags with an accessory light to make seeing hits easier. These are the basic tips for setting tip-ups. For more tip-up advice, be sure to read the pike chapter (Chapter 12).

Wrap Up

Walleye are a worthy winter adversary for ice anglers. Their moderate activity level and swaying winter disposition from aggressive to extremely fussy offers a mix of challenge and action over the entire winter season—not to mention that walleye are one of the best-tasting freshwater fish out there. In the next chapter, we'll look at another one of my top winter species: yellow perch.

YELLOW PERCH

YELLOW PERCH

When perch are active, the fishing can be so fun-filled that hooking a fish with each drop of a lure can be common... until the school swims away. Of course, the action isn't always non-stop and multiple moves happen, especially if chasing jumbos, but overall perch are tough to beat for being willing biters, scrappy fighters, and tasty on the table. In this chapter, I'll show you where to look for perch and how to catch them. Many jigging tactics for walleye I describe in Chapter 8 can be adjusted slightly for perch; so here I'll focus on perch specifics and time-honored tactics.

SPECIES SUMMARY

The yellow perch is part of the same family of fish (Perch) as walleye. Perch are easily distinguished by a series of vertically tapering bars that run down their sides. These bars range in color from shades of olive-green to light and dark browns that match the color of the fish's back. Between these bars, perch are a golden yellow, sometimes with hints of green mixed in. The upper fins are often dark, while lower fins can be orange to red.

Perch are considered a cool-water fish and remain quite active in winter. They inhabit a variety of environments, but do best in lakes and rivers with adequate vegetation, fairly clear water, and gravel, sand, or soft-bottom zones.

Yellow perch also school, which means that if you can catch one, you can usually get more. Another characteristic of perch (to their detriment but to the benefit of anglers) is that they're a curious and competitive species. They're regularly attracted to lures and if you can get enough perch looking at your bait, it's often only a matter of time before you can get one to strike.

For the most part, perch are daytime feeders biting from sunrise to sundown. During the night, they're fairly inactive and rest on the bottom, no doubt to avoid the appetites of twilight hunters like walleye, but also because they have poor vision in low light conditions. On some lakes, jumbo perch over 12-inches actually behave like walleye, hunting on expansive flats as twilight sets in to feed on a variety of tiny organisms. As perch regularly feed throughout winter, they never stray too far from their food sources.

Paul Nelson with a chunky perch.
Photo: Noel Vick.

Depending on the make-up of a lake and what they're eating, perch may inhabit deep water over 30 feet or swim the shallows in less than 5 feet.

Perch themselves feed on a variety of food items. This includes aquatic insects like chironomidae or midge larvae (also called bloodworms), invertebrates like fresh water shrimp (also called scuds) or crayfish, and minnows or juvenile fish, like bluegills and even perch. On the other hand, the yellow perch also serves as prey for walleye, pike, and lake trout. Learning the winter location of yellow perch not only yields good action for anglers, but is often a window into the whereabouts of larger predators as well.

FINDING YELLOW PERCH BENEATH THE ICE

Perch are wandering feeders, munching on various types of food throughout the day. But while they do roam, their movements aren't haphazard. Sometimes you can locate schools relatively easily with an understanding of the underwater make-up of the lake, but on most days the recipe for success is drilling a lot of holes and fishing plenty of water until you find them. Once you find perch though, you can often get them to bite with the right strategy. The question is whether they're aggressive and willing to chase baits, or if you'll need a finesse approach to get bites.

> *Finding Perch* 〉〉
>
> *The keys to perch fishing are to keep moving until you find fish, be efficient when you find them, and be smart and figure out why the perch are where they are so you can find other similar areas with fish.*
>
> Paul Nelson, Ice Fishing Guide, MN

This jumbo perch was feeding on bloodworms living in the muck of a 25-foot flat.

Perch may be found in shallow or deep areas throughout the ice fishing season, with midwinter being the phase where they're most likely to hover in deeper zones. Perch will also hold at various depths within the water column throughout the winter. Whether tight to bottom or suspended, their whereabouts have a lot to do with their food source (see Food Factor).

At the start of the ice season, look for perch in the vicinity of healthy weeds in lakes or areas out of the main-channel current in rivers. Bays, slow-tapering drop-offs near weed lines, soft-bottom zones, flats, or expansive humps are all areas to try. If the weed beds are dead, you're best off moving away from the shoreline towards the base of drop-offs or on deeper sand and gravel bars. Ice fishing guru and guide, Brian "Bro" Brosdahl of Max, Minnesota notes finding chara (sandgrass) can lead to good perch action. Chara grows in sand and gravel areas. The weed sometimes grows in clumps up to a foot or so off the lake floor, giving bottom an irregular shape. When a lake has a lot of flats, these type of vegetation contours are really important to finding perch, he says. Perch will hold around the green stuff all day rooting around for crayfish and small minnows. Chara makes great cover, so look for it when sight fishing clear water or with an underwater camera.

Steve Barnett with two late-ice perch taken from a weed clump on a sandy flat.

In midwinter, perch are often deeper. This is when soft-bottom flats and humps shine. Deep-water perch fishing is a game of working lots of water to try and find fish on vast areas. It's best to begin your search at the base of the last drop off where the deep water begins, depending on the size and type of lake this could be 20 to 40 feet. For the most part perch concentrate on soft-bottom areas that hold a variety of aquatic insects and worms that will sustain them during the winter.

"Perch like to be in the mud during the winter, with the ideal locations close to or between structures so perch have the option to supplement their insects with some minnows and crayfish from harder-bottomed areas closer to structure. The best locations have the right type of mud to support insects - harder sticky mud, rather than soft loon-poop type mud - in close proximity to structure. I like a series of mud humps or harder bottomed humps surrounded by deep water with the right kind of mud," says ice fishing guide Paul Nelson of Bemidji, Minnesota. I share Nelson's view on flats between structure; one of my top midwinter perch spots is a 30 foot flat occurring between two islands, which is near the deepest basin area on a 850 acre lake. I've caught perch feeding on bloodworms on the flat as well as juvenile sport fish, like bluegills.

Jason Mitchell, a guide with Perch Patrol on Devil's Lake, North Dakota spends a lot of time chasing perch on expansive areas. He even mounts his Vexilar to the dash of his vehicle so he can cover a lot of water to try and find nomadic jumbos. "The frustrating part of it is, when perch are running big expansive flats, they can be anywhere. 'It's the guy who drills the most holes that wins' is what we always say. But there are structures to key in on, and they're really subtle things most folks overlook," he notes.

One of these subtle changes could be a switch in bottom composition from muck or sand to a large gravel bed that rises up a foot. Mitchell sees these transition areas on flats like a fence in a pasture. Just like cows relate to the fence, perch will follow the edge of these transition areas, often collecting in the corners. "Transition areas can be anywhere on a flat, but they can corner fish and stall them, funneling them into a tighter area... generally making them easier to catch [than scattered ones]."

Subtle dips in depth on deep flats of at least a foot can also collect fish. Depressions are natural settling areas for lake debris, says Brosdahl. On a sticky mud bottom this organic material is a buffet for bloodworms. Dips and dimples in flats concentrate this important perch forage and attract jumbos.

Brian "Bro" Brosdahl with a spoon-fooled jumbo. Photo: Noel Vick.

Focus on flats on lakes for midwinter perch. In rivers, explore deeper areas out of the main river current, such as holes in backwater zones, bays, or off-channel flats.

Luckily, as late ice arrives, perch location becomes more predictable. As spring-spawners, perch migrate to the shallows as late ice arrives. Look for perch on shallow, weedy flats and around slow-tapering transitions into vegetation-rich or reedy, wood-strewn bays. Again, pinpointing variations in an otherwise uniform bottom will concentrate fish. On many shallow flats I fish during late ice, sand patches among newly growing weeds will often concentrate perch. I can often spot them by gazing down the hole in clear water systems. Perch will travel along the sand-weed edge and working a bait in the open area on or off bottom will get a roaming school's attention.

Location Nuances: The Food Factor

Beyond knowing that the areas mentioned above may hold perch, another major factor in determining their whereabouts is food. Ample forage dictates perch location. The challenge becomes finding perch when they're roaming for a meal. If they're feasting on burrowing insects, be prepared to pluck them off soft-bottom areas. These areas could be large flats or the bottom of breaks close to the main basin. Crayfish are another impor-

tant source of food, especially for big perch. As noted earlier chara can hold craws, as will sand and weed zones. If they're chomping on scuds or minnows, you'll likely find them near bays or weedy flats.

I've lost count of the number of times I've cut dozens of ice holes and spent hours fishing on a quest to locate perch on a new lake. Then, often within a few yards of a hole that had no activity at all, suddenly my sonar lights up and I've found the school. In many instances, the reason fish are where they are is food.

What's also important to understand is perch will act differently depending on what their eating. A school of jumbos chasing minnows are often aggressive and take the shape of a hunting pack, with perch out to the sides and on top of each other. These fish will often crush spoons or jigging minnows. This is a sharp contrast from those grazing on bottom-dwelling bloodworms, where schools often spread out on bottom, and usually demand smaller baits and a delicate jigging approach. In clear water situations you can sometimes see perch swimming and watch whether they're feeding on bottom or suspended. Watching your portable sonar in deeper water for fish signals and interpreting the whereabouts of perch in the water column gives you clues on what they're feeding on and their level of activity.

> ### *Pillage and Plunder* »
>
> *It takes a lot of fuel to feed a big school of perch. They are like an invading hoard of barbarians; they pillage and plunder everything in sight and then move on to other areas with better feeding opportunities."*
>
> Paul Nelson, Ice Fishing Guide, MN

Juvenile fish are frequently on the menu in winter. The profile and color of this Northland Forage Minnow Spoon proved an adequate stunt double to fool this perch.

FINDING AND STAYING ON A SCHOOL: TEAM FISHING 101

I've mentioned that finding perch can be challenging because they often roam large areas throughout the day. Locating perch demands patience. Working together as a group to fish different depths and structures shortens your overall search time, helping you pinpoint a school's coordinates. A group of four anglers or more cooperating in pairs (each with an auger) can quickly cover a lot of water with search lures. Having a lake map and taking time to plan your attack is well worth it. Not only does planning your search make you more efficient, it's a great reward when everything comes together and you get on a school. Common tactics may include having some anglers start deep, while others start shallow on a long point or a sloping flat, or zigzagging in pairs across a bar or a deep hole. If you have access to snow machines, splitting up to explore different areas completely and staying in contact with portable radios is another perch-hunting tactic. Once you find fish, signal to the other anglers in your fishing party to join in on the action. Having several baits in the area will keep the school's attention.

As much as you should be prepared to fish tightly together to keep a school's interest, you also need to be ready to travel to follow perch when they move. There's nothing wrong with a lazy day on the ice with family and friends on structures that have proven themselves as perch zones, but it can be a gamble if you simply kick back and wait for fish to return after they've left. Sometimes perch don't come back, especially on big water. For this reason, it's worthwhile to drill plenty of holes and to try to follow them. As the action subsides, spread out in different directions, fishing a variety of holes to try to determine the pack's direction. To follow a school, you need to be mobile: have portable shelters and pack light.

Plenty of moves and drilling lots of holes are part of the game when searching for quality perch and being able to follow the school when it moves.

JIGGING TACTICS FOR YELLOW PERCH

Jigging is definitely the most common tactic for perch fishing. Carry a mix of large lures for searching as well as finesse baits to be prepared. On certain days, spoons and jigging minnows take the biggest perch while on other days you'll need to finesse them, in which case smaller jigs may work better. As I've already described the different types of jigging lures in the walleye chapter (Chapter 8), let's focus here on what to choose and how to use them to catch yellow perch.

Spoons and Jigging Minnows

Spoons put out a lot of flash and vibrations. Bent spoons, gliders, and straight models all have their place for perch. Top choices for perch include smaller, 1- to 2-inch versions of the baits mentioned in the walleye chapter (Chapter 8).

Jigging minnows are also excellent choices for perch. The circling glide of these baits can call in perch from quite a distance. The profile on these lures also does well to fool perch into biting. Fish these baits on similar jigging sequences as you would for walleye. Tipping one hook with bait will give perch a target, but even nude lures will enchant jumbos to eat.

As a general rule, when I start fishing I use a large, rattling spoon that puts out a lot of flash and noise to call in fish. I'm looking for big, active, feeding fish willing to hit a large offering. Big spoons also appeal to large, aggressive perch. If fish are biting consistently, but you're not getting the size you're hoping for, upgrading to a larger-sized lure can sometimes help you weed-out the pint-sized perch and coax the jumbos to chow down. The other benefit to large spoons is that they're heavier,

> ### Loose the Line Twist »
>
> *When you're jigging aggressively [with spoons] you're working a lot of twist in the line. If it spins when you have to scale back and hold the lure still or bob it, you're not going to catch as many fish, so I use a swivel... tied about a foot or so above the lure.*
>
> Jason Mitchell, Ice Fishing Guide and Rod Designer, ND

Sue Butchart plucks another perch from a soft-bottom flat.

The author with a perch taken on a Northland Puppet Minnow.

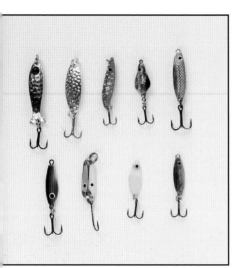

A selection of spoons that work well for perch (and crappie). Top row: JB Lures Angel Eye, Williams Wabler, Blue Fox Rattle Flash Jigging Spoon, Lindy Rattl'n Flyer Spoon, Northland Buck-Shot Rattle Spoon. Bottom Row: JB Lures Varmit, Jig-A-Whopper Hawger Spoon, Lindy Frostee Jigging Spoon, and Northland Forage Minnow Spoon.

making them ideal for fishing in deeper water. This also lets you get down quickly to biting perch and catch several to delay them slightly before their inevitable move.

If I'm not having success, I switch to a smaller lure. I'll use models around an inch when fish are finicky or neutral (often the case during midwinter) or in clear water situations when they will scrutinize baits more. Smaller-sized spoons can also outperform larger baits when perch live in water bodies with a lot of forage and can be more selective. Baits this size are best when you've located fish and need to trigger them into biting. If I'm attracting fish with spoons but I can't get bites, I change rods and switch to a dropper rig or jig.

Dropper Rigs

Dropper rigs are a hybrid between spoons or jigging minnows and ice jigs. Essentially, a dropper rig is fashioned by removing the treble on either of these lures and attaching a small section of line (often 2- to 6-inches) to which a small baited ice jig or hook is tied.

The spoon or jigging minnow serves as the attractor. The dropper appeals to finicky fish unwilling to hit large baits but that are susceptible to the temptation of a tiny morsel that can be easily slurped up. The added bonus to this rig is its weight, which makes it excellent for fishing deeper water as they sink quickly. Good droppers include: ice flies, vertical or horizontal ice jigs, or plain hooks tipped with live or soft baits.

Jig these baits as you would a regular spoon, but include plenty of quivers and pauses to let the pint-sized dropper do its job. Tipped with fresh scent from live maggots or artificial bait, the smaller offering is often too tempting to pass up for a semi-curious perch intrigued by the flash and flutter of the larger lure. You can also run dropper rigs using two ice jigs; I cover this tactic in the crappie chapter (Chapter 10)

Ice Jigs

Sometimes, you need to go small to tempt the jumbos. It could be because fish are keying-in on micro-sized food such as tiny bloodworms or fresh-water shrimp. Or it might be that they're inactive and the best chance of fooling them is with a small ice jig tipped with several, juicy maggots, a waxworm, or a soft-bait teaser tail.

Another benefit to ice jigs is that they only feature one hook. This is a plus because when the perch bite is on, you want to be able to hook and quickly unhook fish. If you're messing around removing trebles, you might cause the school to lose interest in your lure and move on. It may sound odd, but keeping your bait in the water and in front of the snouts of curious perch is the best way to prolong a bite of aggressive fish. Ice jigs come in a variety of sizes and weights and those used for perch will also catch crappie and sunfish. Any of the ice jigs from the Northland Bro's Bug Collection will work, as will the Lindy Genz Bug, Fat Boys, and Frostee, JB Lures Hot-Heads and Big Max, and Custom Jigs and Spins Diamond Jig and Demon Perch Eye. Various jigs by Maynards and Little Atom will also take perch.

A spoon and vertical ice jig set-up is just one of the many dropper combinations that will fool fussy perch.

Of course, the range of ice jigs extends beyond weighted hooks with fancy color patterns. Some ice jigs have spinner blades integrated into their design, like the Northland Whistler Jig or JB Lures Charmers. These blades emit vibrations on the lift and fall of jigging sequences and can sometimes coax big perch to hit when standard jigs aren't working. Stock your ice-tackle box with these baits for variety.

Tiny plastic or soft-bait jigging lures are also highly effective on perch. A major advantage of plastics and soft baits is they don't need to be rebaited between fish, letting you get your bait quickly back down the hole before the school leaves. They can also be shaped to accurately mimic different fishy food items. Plus, plastics won't freeze when hole hopping, which is a disadvantage of live bait.

For these reasons, on my perch outings at least one of my rods will be rigged with a soft bait. I'm a big fan of small tubes, of about 1- to 1.5-inches in length, like the Northland Slurpies Small Fry or Berkley PowerBait Atomic Tubes. There's something about a white tube that really appeals to perch. In addition to tubes, there are some other soft baits on the market worth considering. The Northland Bro's Bloodworm or Berkley Fish Fry do well to imitate midge larvae, while the Northland Scud Bug is a great replica of freshwater shrimp and their Mimic Minnow Fry copies various young of the year fish. Perch are cannibalistic. Sometimes fishing with a perch colored plastic can catch you a lot of jumbos. All of these morsels are regular food items for perch and it's wise to bring some imitations to be prepared.

Jack Levert lands a jumbo perch fooled by the flickering tail action and realistic profile of a Northland Scud Bug.

Baiting Up

Tipping lures to bolster their taste and smell will help you ice more perch over the season. Bait spoons and jigging minnows with minnows as you would for walleye. Small minnow heads and tails tipped on treble or single hooks work well.

Maggots and waxworms are dynamite baits to use for tipping spoons for perch. Small, 1-inch spoons can become even more effective when combined with a bit of scent. The crappie chapter (Chapter 10) in this book has a section on tipping baits with maggots and waxies that can also be used here.

Although real bait is excellent for finessing fish, scent-infused soft bait can also be used for various lures. Berkley has a variety of good products for tipping ice jigs. Top choices include their Gulp! Maggots and Waxies. I pack a few of these items in the pockets of my rod carrier case so that they're always on hand.

Whether you use real or artificial bait, tipping spoons, jigging minnows, or jigs boosts the appeal of the lure. This gives fish a visual and scent target, encouraging them to bite the hook, as opposed to striking the head of the jig, which unfortunately does happen at times when they're biting light. I've experimented while sight fishing shallow water and it's amazing how often perch will peck at the head of a horizontal jig. Add some bait and the hook instantly becomes a tantalizing bull's-eye, boosting your hook-up rates. For this reason too, it's sometimes best to use a vertical jig instead of a horizontal one.

Perch Jigging Tips

Here are some jigging moves that I've found particularly useful for perch:

1. Sequences incorporating a lot of movement, like wrist snaps can do well to attract perch. My sight fishing experience with perch reveals that unless they're very aggressive, perch often first come in and stare at lures. Then, once they gather and circle around a bait, their competitiveness kicks in and often you can trick one of them to strike. Pauses and subtle shakes help encourage these hits.

2. When perch are neutral or inactive, slowing down is often the best way to get bites. When manipulating ice jigs, you become a puppeteer, working an artificial bait in an attempt to pass it off as a small minnow, shrimp, worm, or other aquatic tidbit. Be careful not to overwork

these tiny baits so that they'll appear natural. If perch aren't interested in hitting ice jigs on lift-fall-pause sequences, begin by controlling these moves more by raising and lowering them on tight line to slow down the rise and drop speeds. Micro-movements, like small hops and swimming sequences, are equally effective.

3. My friend, Jack Levert, is a perch fanatic and often describes his finesse jigging as a "soft, pulsating motion". This is a good phrase to keep in mind when working ice jigs because you don't want your moves to be jerky or erratic but rather natural, fluid, and lifelike.

4. Fish spoons and jigging minnows as described for walleye on lift-fall-pause sequences. Subtle moves like quivers or jiggles combined with frequent pauses are fruitful triggering moves.

5. Another effective tactic to provoke strikes is slowly moving baits up and away from fish you've marked on your sonar. This maneuver forces perch to chase and bite or let a meal get away.

6. Whatever lure you're using, don't always let it freefall to the floor; instead, dance the bait down the bottom half of the water column. Doing this catches suspending fish and aggressive perch that will rise off the bottom to hit the falling offering.

7. Banging your bait on bottom is another tactic. This kicks up a silt cloud, mimics bottom-feeding activity, and attracts curious perch. Before raising jigs off bottom, try this first: move the bait ever-so-slightly, keeping it on bottom, while mixing in pauses of a few seconds. Big perch eat a lot of small crayfish and dancing a small lure on a soft bottom can be enough to mimic these crustaceans and instigate strikes. This bottom-dancing trick is best done with ice jigs, but it's sometimes effective with larger offerings, like spoons.

Perch Jigging Sticks

Light to medium-light power rods with fast or extra-fast action between 28- to 36-inches work well for perch. Dipping below this length may be beneficial when sight-fishing for perch or if in cramped quarters. Four-pound-test nylon or fluorocarbon line is the bread-and-butter of your perch combos. Bumping up to 6-pound-test is a good idea if you're targeting jumbos near points and reefs where you might intercept the occasional walleye, or during those bonanza bites when jumbos go crazy. Conversely, drop to 2-or 3-pound-test line when perch are fussy or in clear water situations.

Finding yellow perch can be challenging but remember to keep moving and drill lots of holes - never give up, no matter how warm the sun and comfy the ice.

SETLINE TACTICS

When the perch are biting, fishing with setlines might result in more fishing action than you can handle. But if you're finding that it takes a finesse approach to produce results, setlines can ice you more perch each outing.

I find that perch, like walleye, are sometimes attracted to a spoon or a jigging minnow but can be reluctant to bite the moving bait. Having a dead-stick rod set near my jigging hole is one way to fool the occasional shy fish.

For jumbo perch, try small minnows hooked behind the dorsal fin with a thin wire hook. An ice jig tipped with a few maggots is another choice. Frequently rebaiting the jig keeps the offering full of scent. Also, keep the rod within reach so that you can give it the occasional lift and quickly set the hook. When dead-sticking for perch, or any panfish, use a float or a noodle rod to signal strikes.

ICE ANGLING ESSENTIALS ⟫

MULTI-SPECIES ADVENTURES

In this book, I separate the how-to content by species, but it's common to hook different types of fish out of the same hole or over the course of the day. In shallow areas, it's not unlikely to catch sunfish, crappie, perch, pike, and sometimes even largemouth bass from the same general area. This of course is great when it happens by accident, but you can also intentionally target different species on a single outing on the same or different water systems. For example, your day could start before dawn by setting up to target some walleye, and then switch over to perch. As day feeders, yellow perch can be a great species to chase as part of a multi-species outing. If the walleye weren't cooperating in the morning, perhaps the evening should be reserved for crappie or bluegills, as the big fish of these species often feed heavily at dusk. Diversifying in this way can make your outings a lot more interesting and deliver better overall catch rates.

Wrap Up

Yellow perch make for a fun and exciting ice angling adventure. They're entertaining to target with children or newbies who'll love catching these spunky fish—and if they're fans of eating fish, they'll love it even more if you end the day with a tasty fish fry.

CRAPPIE

CRAPPIE

Most ice anglers have a bittersweet relationship with crappie. When you find an active school, the fishing can be outstanding. Yet on other days, locating them seems next to impossible. For serious fishers, the crappie's sporadically elusive nature is incentive enough to try catching them. Just as appealing is their succulent, white flakey meat. This chapter explains where to find winter crappie, what lures to use, and strategies to land big slabs.

SPECIES SUMMARY

Black crappie have green or golden-brown backs and heads with green to shiny silver sides mixed with clusters of black spots. White crappie have green to black backs and heads, and their sides are silver in color with green undertones behind loose vertical bars. Black crappie are more commonly targeted through the ice given their wider distribution, but targeting both species is very similar.

Crappie are considered cool-water fish, which means that they're fairly active throughout winter. These fish tend to hold in loose schools, which is good news for ice anglers because it means that once you find one crappie, there are usually others in the vicinity. But don't expect crappie to make it easy for you; often fussy and regularly suspending in the water, these fish will test your angling skills to the limit.

Crappie feed on a variety of items. They'll munch on fish, including minnows and juvenile panfish, aquatic insects, and invertebrates. Crappie will also use their fine gill rakers to sift through the water and feed on zooplankton.

FINDING CRAPPIE BENEATH THE ICE

At first ice, crappie may be scattered in a variety of areas on lakes. On small, fertile lakes that are the first to freeze up, expect to find crappie relating to the deepest hole where they might hold tight to bottom or be suspended up several feet. On larger lakes crappie often slide to steep

The business end of a black crappie.

breaks leading to mid-depth flats or deep-basin areas. They hold in deep water areas near structures like points, humps, or the base of a drop off where it meets the basin. Areas where large bays meet the main lake can also be hot spots at early ice. If large enough, deep holes inside these bays can hold fish at ice up. In rivers, look for crappie to move out of the main channel to backwater areas, like bays, canals, or harbors. Crappie often spend the entire winter in these spots to avoid the river's current, but also because the locations hold food. Rivers in general are underutilized but are good year-round bets for crappie.

Midwinter crappie fishing on lakes is often a game of probing deep basin areas. At this point in winter, weeds have died off and their decomposition zaps oxygen from the shallows, so larger bodies of water are better bets than shallow, fertile spots. Crappie may also move deeper to find warmer water. Cold water is less dense and occurs beneath the ice and in shallow areas, while warm water is denser and sinks to deeper zones. Crappies and other panfish follow the more "temperate" winter water and inhabit deeper areas. Fish won't just roam these regions, they'll relate to structures. Using lake maps to find humps, long bars, or island points jutting into deep water is a good midwinter crappie strategy.

> ### Panfish Diet »
>
> *Panfish eat a lot more critters than they do baitfish. Far more than many anglers realize. Whether it's picking crustaceans out of weeds, or gorging on the infinite types of zooplankton and other creepy-crawly things that go beyond bloodworms and mayfly larvae. Foodstuffs like these things are slow-moving, readily available, and tend to be concentrated in the winter.*
>
> Noel Vick, Ice Fishing Expert and Outdoor Journalist, MN

Tim Allard with proof that rivers are crappie hotspots.

My regular ice fishing chum, Jack Levert, often uses the phrase "activating a school" when we're fishing an area we know holds inactive perch, crappie, or sunfish. The goal is to be patient but be persistent when jigging to get fish interested and looking. As more fish gather their competitive nature takes over and, when successful, eventually one of them breaks down and bites. Once you've activated the school they're morphed from a pack of non-violent protestors refusing to bite your bait to an aggressive mob ready to rip your lure to pieces. Once you land the first one, the important thing is to get your bait back down the hole to keep fish stimulated before the feeding frenzy subsides. In most situations fast and steady jigging with small ice jigs works best. For perch and crappie another trick is upsizing to a larger spoon or jigging minnow to rile up fish and get the first bite. After the larger lure's charisma wanes, lowering an ice jig can seduce a few more strikes.

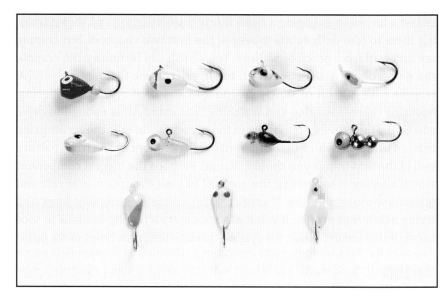

A series of ice jigs for crappie that will also take yellow perch and bluegill. The top row (left to right) are Custom Jigs and Spins Diamond Jig, HT Enterprises Marmooska, Northland Mud Bug, and Lindy Genz Bug. The middle row (left to right) are Northland Gill Getter and Bro Bug, JB Lures Hot Head, and Lindy Genz Worm. The bottom row (left to right) are vertical / teardrop jigs including JB Lures Candy Cane, Custom Jigs and Spins 2 Spot, and Lindy Frostee.

zontal jigs when crappie are inactive. A lot of this has to do with the slow fall of these light jigs combined with the jig's profile that better matches their forage. Of course, once you figure out the color, size, and jigging pattern, the action's often more consistent.

An effective way to determine crappie lure preferences is using a dual ice jig dropper rig. One way to make the rig is to tie on a vertical ice jig with a polamer knot. Doing this turns the vertical jig into a horizontally hanging one, so make sure the hook points up, leave a long tag end and then affix your second jig (either horizontal or vertical). Another trick is to tie on a horizontal jig designed with a collar, like a Northland Bro Bug or Lindy Genz Worm. Next tie the dropper line around the ice jig's collar with a loop or improved clinch knot. Then add your second ice jig to the dropper line. This lower jig should be the heavier to avoid tangling on the fall. Spacing between droppers can vary, but 8- to 15-inches is often best. Fish these droppers as you would a stand-alone ice jig. Not only do droppers let you offer different sizes, profiles, and colors of bait to fish, but the vertical separation between them helps you probe more of the water column, an added bonus when searching for suspending crappie.

Tips on Working Ice Jigs

When fishing ice jigs for crappie, begin with small hops by quickly lifting or flicking the rod tip. This calls in aggressive fish. When fish are neutral or inactive, subtle or pulsating jigging moves tend to be better than aggressive ones. Also remember that crappie often feed on tiny invertebrates, so less movement is often best. Small shaking hand movements translate to a nervous jiggle in baits. The trembling keeps the jig looking small, alive, and tempting enough to eat. Quivering mixed with pauses, rod raises, and side-to-side movements gives you an array of jigging techniques to try on selective fish. To be successful at this presentation, don't overdo it. For

Subtle quivers of a maggot-tipped horizontal ice jig fooled this 13-inch crappie for the author. Photo: Serge Bricault.

St. Croix's Legend Ice spring bobber rod helped Sue Butchart swim a jig to fool this crappie.

the most part, concentrate on just barely moving your hand. If you focus on the rod tip you'll likely overwork the bait. As movements only need to be slight, hold the rod in a pencil grip position. Not only is this more comfortable over a full day, but it helps with extremely subtle movements. It also makes hooks sets as easy as snapping the wrist.

Another excellent tactic when finesse fishing with tiny ice jigs is working baits through the water column. When doing this, I try to mimic a swimming aquatic insect. I like to think of the saying "two steps forward, one step back" for this presentation style. While jiggling the rod ever so slightly, slowly raise the tip upwards. Do this to move the jig up a few inches and then continue to rocker the rod as you drop it down half-way before pausing and then lifting it again. When doing this type of micro-move, a spring bobber or noodle rod gives the offering a natural, smooth motion. I've found this tactic particularly effective on finicky crappie. They might not want to eat a bait hopping or staying still at the same depth, yet start to swim the snack away and it's amazing how rapidly their appetite returns.

Remember fish moods vary and so there's no such thing as a surefire angling presentation. As I've said before, the chief challenge and joy of ice angling comes from the variability, and when it comes to jigging moves you'll find experimentation pays off.

Baiting Up

In the walleye chapter (Chapter 8), I covered details on using minnows for ice fishing. Tipping spoons and jigging minnows with a piece of minnow tail or head works for large or aggressive crappie. Small, live minnows rigged on ice jigs are another time-proven presentation; I'll discuss this in the setline section.

Maggots are extremely popular for tipping lures for panfish. Euro larvae maggots come dyed in various colors or in their natural shade of plain off-white with a hint of yellow. These fly larvae squirm and wiggle if hooked properly, adding movement to a lure, while emitting flavorful juices and scent. Barely hook maggots at their blunt end with two small dots. Light hooking in this area keeps maggots alive and wiggling in the ice-cold water. Typically, anglers use two to three maggots on ice jigs – but there's no magic number, so be sure to try other combinations.

Waxworms are another baiting option. "Waxies make a mess in the water and draw in fish," says ice fishing icon, Brian "Bro" Brosdahl of

Max, Minnesota. "In crowded fishing situations, I'll sometimes gob on a bunch of waxies to put out a scent trail and a puff cloud." In less populated fishing areas simply threading a waxworm on a hook shank will work. Bro's also a fan of head hooking a waxworm and then squeezing out the innards. The remaining flap of skin holds fresh scent and tantalizingly dances when the jig is quivered.

To make rigging with larvae easy, keep hook points sharp so you can easily pierce the bait without tearing it. Sometimes pinching down or filing off a portion of the barb also helps.

Crappie Jigging Sticks

Light and ultra-light power rods between 24- to 36-inches are well suited for crappie. Remember to match the rod to the weight of the lure. I highly recommend that at least one of your outfits has a spring bobber or is a noodle rod. I've already noted how these devices help give a swimming action to ice jigs. They're also critical for detecting light-biting crappie. Crappie frequently grab ice jigs and swim up with them. Unless you're extremely in-tune with the characteristics of your fishing line, you'll miss

Rebaiting »»

Rebaiting is critical to catching fish as freshness often stimulates hits. If others are out-fishing you and they're adding fresh bait after five minutes, this is a sign to speed up your baiting tempo. When fish are hot, you can extend the timeframe, but when they're finicky, adding fresh bait frequently is best.

these hits. A properly set-up spring bobber or noodle rod, on the other hand, is always slightly bent under the weight of the jig. When a crappie hits and swims up with a jig, the spring or rod tip straightens, signaling the hit. Also, when a fish takes a bait gently, these ultra-sensitive devices flicker or drop just a hair to give away the strike.

I spool reels with 3- to 4-pound-test line for heavier offerings and when crappie are aggressively feeding. Two-pound-test is recommended for clear water, fickle fish, and when presenting ultra-light, micro lures.

SETLINE TACTICS

Dead-sticking a secondary line when setting up on a known crappie spot is an excellent way to catch some extra fish. Stationary lines are also beneficial for hooking crappie you've attracted to the area through jigging. Often a maggot- or waxworm-tipped ice jig a short distance away will get a hit if the spoon's not doing the job.

Dead-sticking small minnows can appeal to slabs. Nose- or back-hooked minnows with ice jigs is one option. Yet sometimes it's better to use a thin, bare hook and then place a tiny split shot a few inches above the minnow. Don't overweight your offering; crappie will detect it. Use a spring bobber or a noodle rod specifically designed with an ultra-sensitive tip for dead-sticking to help you spot hits on dead-stick lines. Another option is using a small float. Avoid the pitfall of using too large of a float and be sure to weight your line with enough split shots so the bobber easily slips beneath the surface when a fish hits. Keep a watchful eye on your dead-stick float. If it sinks, raises, or twitches, set the hook. Ensure the rod is within reach too so you can give it the occasional lift to attract fish, but also so you can grab it quickly and bring in the biter.

Night Fishing for Crappie

Crappie are often active at twilight and into the night. Fish that were suspending off of structures or in the basin during the day can suddenly materialize in numbers on humps, points, and weedlines. When you're night fishing, expect crappie to suspend anywhere from a foot or two off-bottom, in the middle of the water column, or just beneath the ice, so sonar is important to your success.

Keep things simple when night fishing. More gear often means more problems and increases the chances of losing something in the dark. I bring a couple rods, a headlamp, and sometimes a small lantern or larger

Steve Barnett cranes in a crappie during a hot bite on a snowy January evening.

ICE ANGLING ESSENTIALS ⟫⟫⟫

THE POWER OF PIECES

Fishing a new lake can be intimidating and staring at a big lake map can get the angling butterflies going. To prevent yourself from being overwhelmed once you hit the ice, try the following. Do a bit of homework first and study a lake map. Break the lake up into quadrants. Then analyze those sections as individual systems and look for areas where you might find your target species. Then do the same for the other sections. Get your fishing buddies involved too and have them do the same. Then pick a section of water to fish. Don't succumb to the siren's call of distant shorelines or points if things get tough, focus on the piece of water you chose for the day and learn its intricacies. If you're fishing with a sizable team, maybe break up to try different zones. Then regardless of the fishing action, whether gangbusters or dismal, return to the lake again and fish its other areas. In the long run, multiple days spent on the same body of water will provide you with a better outdoor education when it comes to fish-catching tactics than aimlessly wandering from one lake to another trying to predict the next hot bite.

light. Arrive and get set up before sunset. Also, collect or organize most of your gear before it gets too dark.

Gathering together some friends for a night fish and staking out known hotspots is a great way to catch a meal and enjoy each other's company. Night crappie fishing is one of the things I look forward to the most at the start of each hard-water season. Crisp night air, biting fish, and jokes among buddies – it's tough to ask for anything else in a great outdoors experience.

Wrap Up

Crappie fishing can be gangbusters, frustrating, and everything in between. These loosely-schooling suspenders can challenge the best ice anglers, but once you find them, the fishing can be fantastic. Remember to experiment with your lures and jigging sequences until you're confident you've found the best fish-catching pattern.

SUNFISH

SUNFISH

When it comes to ice fishing, the two most popular sunfish are bluegills and pumpkinseeds. These colorful and spunky fish put up impressive tussles on ultra-light gear. Small fish are often easy to find year-round, but patterning trophy-sized 'gills or 'seeds takes time and know-how.

SPECIES SUMMARY

Considered warm-water fish, bluegills and pumpkinseeds still remain active during the winter months. The two species have similar, deep-body types.

In terms of color, pumpkinseeds have green or brown backs, with golden-brown to olive sides clad with spots. Their color lightens from top to bottom and their heads have strands of horizontal stripes in a variety of hues of blue and green. Their ear-flap is black with a red spot.

Bluegills also have greenish-brown backs and loose vertical bands extending down their sides. Their ear-flap is black.

Sunfish feed on a variety of items. Although pint-sized, these fish are active predators. For the most part, sunfish eat a range of insect larvae, aquatic invertebrates, crustaceans, zooplankton, and plant material. What this means is that small ice jigs are the go-to baits for serious sunfish pursuers. Sunfish also school, so once you find them you should be able to hook several.

FINDING SUNFISH BENEATH THE ICE

At first ice, look for sunfish in healthy weedbed areas. These lush underwater forests provide cover and protection from predators, but also hold a range of tiny food items. Top ice spots on lakes include sheltered bays, slow-tapering flats, beside bullrush shorelines, around islands, and weed-covered humps and points. Big panfish are edge oriented, so expect to find them around weed walls and in pockets or cuts in vegetation.

Small ponds and pits are good early-ice panfish spots. Look for them in the greenery as well as the deepest holes and depressions in the pond's bottom. For the majority of the winter in rivers, panfish will hold in bays, inlets, tributaries, and backwater areas. In addition to weeds, sunken timber and stumps will attract fish.

A bluegill

During midwinter, panfish location varies depending on the water body. There is a shift away from the shallow, vegetation-rich zones that held fish at first ice on lakes. As these weedbeds die and the shallows become colder, fish move deeper. At midwinter, several types of cover will hold panfish. Smaller fish may still continue to lurk in the shallow areas mentioned above but deep weedbeds will also hold sunfish, especially if the plant stalks remain standing to provide cover. Other areas to look for sunfish are mid to deep flats or near basin areas. The best flats have soft bottoms and are home to a variety of sunfish forage, such as insect larvae. Humps and points will also hold big sunfish during midwinter. In deeper water, sunfish may suspend or hold tight to bottom.

At late ice, sunfish often return to the shallows when weeds begin to grow again as the intensity of the sun and daylight increases. Spring and early summer spawners, sunfish stage near shallow bays, flats, shorelines, and tributaries. During the last two weeks of the ice season, fishing is often fantastic as sunfish congregate in large numbers in shallow areas and feed heavily in preparation for the spawn.

Location Nuances

Sunfish are the diet of larger predators, so these fish often hold tight to cover. When exploring areas like bays, finding cover is important. Healthy green weeds and sunken wood can concentrate panfish in high numbers

The Secret Spot »

At early ice bluegills are often between weed edges and the basin, but by working diligently with your electronics and underwater camera you can seek out small pieces of isolated cover such as weeds, perhaps a few pieces of rock, or - my favorite in Eastern Ontario and most waters I have fished is - an area where the silt is washed off the bottom and exposes firm sandy bottom with pea sized gravel mixed in. This is usually just a little bit shallower than the surrounding bottom and that is why the silt remains washed off...sort of like small firm humps, although they may be only 10-15 feet across, they are primo in this bluegill guy's world. These areas will be quite visible and often contain different colored stones or gravel which is very easy to see on a sunny day if the water is clear or with a camera on other days or lakes where the visibility may be just a wee bit darker.

"Big" Jim McLaughlin, Professional Angler and Publisher of Just Fishing Magazine, ON

"Big" Jim McLaughlin with a bluegill.

under the ice. Be sure to mark attractive looking cover during your pre-ice scouting on a map or GPS unit.

Locating weeds or wood isn't a guarantee of success, though. You still must sift through these areas thoroughly. Drilling several holes is one way to boost your chances of a big 'gill or stout 'seed. This gives you multiple attack points. In my experience, certain holes in the mix always end up being the hot spots. These are often located above prime areas like bends or pockets in weeds. Punching plenty of holes also lets you take more "ice casts" and dunk into more spots through the weeds. This tactic also increases your catches on days when fish won't move far for baits and dropping a jig right on their nose is the only way to get a bite.

When working weeds, divide the water into two parts: above weeds and in them. Swim the jig down till it's just above the weeds. Work it here to get a fish's attention and try and raise one to hit the offering. Sometimes this works, but often you need to dunk the greenery. Fish from the top of the weed canopy to the bottom. Sunfish can be anywhere, so keep a watchful eye on your sonar for fish signals among the weed stalks. Don't waste time in the same spot if you're not marking fish in the weeds and quickly move to the next hole. You'll occasionally get hung up fishing weeds and will need to tear the bait free. Don't get discouraged, it's worth it for the fish you'll catch. It may also take a few tries to penetrate certain areas, and using a heavier jig helps.

A mid-lake hump coughed up this aggressive pumpkinseed.

Also, don't be afraid to venture out beyond the weeds and fish just past the drop off. A few winter's ago I joined "Big" Jim McLaughlin on a bluegill spot he's spent several years fishing. We worked a soft-bottom flat that ranged between 15 to 18 feet. McLaughlin's found the zone where the flat meets an inside turn in the drop-off to be the best area. But it's not just the nuances of this contour that attracts 'gills. It's also because the inside turn cuts into the biggest weed flat on the lake, McLaughlin calls it a food shelf. It's the food found in the weeds and the deeper flat, along with the inside turn and the vast weed cover that all combine to make this area the best spot on the lake.

Locating healthy weeds is a big element to finding sunfish.

Another tip when it comes to fish location: it sometimes pays to leave a hot hole for a while if the bite is slowing. You could be directly above the best rock pile on a mud flat or a pocket in a lush weedbed, but after 15 minutes of hooking sunfish, all but the most aggressive of schools can get skittish. A great tactic is making a short move to fish some of the other holes you've drilled while letting the area settle down before returning. Fish won't stray too far, and on large bays or flats, you can often find multiple hotspots.

This tactic serves me well on one of my favorite late ice spots for bluegills. It's a large sand and soft bottom area that gently slopes from five to 12 feet of water and is in front of two shallow, spawning bays. The bottom is mixed with clumps of weeds and small rock piles. My friends and I will drill dozens of holes upon arriving and quickly work through them. Inevitably the ones drilled above weed edges, pockets, or beside rock piles are frequently the best spots to jig. Once these productive holes are established our days pass by quickly. We simply keep rotating through established areas that are concentrating fish, occasionally cracking "musical chairs" jokes that never seem to get old when we're catching fish. Of course, if the action slows we grab the auger and probe further, or load up and make a major move to try another area completely.

JIGGING TACTICS FOR SUNFISH

Quivering a tiny ice jig with an ultra-light rod while playing cat-and-mouse with a fish on your sonar unit is exciting, especially when the end result rewards you with a big bluegill. For the most part, tiny ice jigs reign supreme when it comes to catching sunfish. I've hooked sunfish on small spoons, but most anglers I know stick to ice jigs when hunting panfish, even when after trophies. Given that I already cover tips for using small

Sue Butchart with a pumpkinseed taken on an ice jig.

Quivering a Northland Gill-Getter tipped with maggots fooled this bluegill.

>>> *Picky 'Gills*

Bluegills have a kind of persnicketiness, a discerning taste for what they will and won't consume... almost like a snobby wine taster. They'll suck in the bait and blow it right back out, tip their chin back, think about whether they want to eat it or if they'll go to the next sampling. This choosiness is amplified in the winter. The water's clearer, fish move slower and, if in fact fish think, they have more time to think about what they're going to hit. There are far fewer reactionary strikes. Bluegills really have to buy-in before they bite, and sometimes the decision to eat or not gets down to taste.

Noel Vick, Ice Fishing Expert and Outdoor Journalist, MN

spoons for perch and crappie, I won't revisit those tactics here. Just remember to use small hooked spoons as sunfish have tiny mouths. Instead, I want to focus on tiny ice jigs as these are the more popular presentations.

In the perch and crappie chapters (Chapters 9 and 10), I discuss the different types of ice jigs available on the market and how vertical, horizontal, and 45- to 60-degree profile baits each have a place in your jig box. I also shared tips on how to work these baits. Now, I want to build on these presentation tactics with some more jigging tips. So, if you skipped right to this chapter, I'd encourage you to review the content on ice jigs in the perch and crappie sections. The Ice Angling Essentials on Jigging in the walleye chapter (Chapter 8) is also worth revisiting.

Ice Jig Tips

At times, sunfish are awfully selective, scrutinizing minute details in jigs. Paying attention to jig profile, color, and movement is important in order to coax hits when fish are neutral. Let's begin with jig profile.

When using horizontal jigs, it's important to ensure the knot is dead center in the line tie. This causes the jig to sit naturally in a horizontal position. After you've hooked and played a fish, the stress of the battle often causes the knot to slide upwards on the line tie. This will alter the profile of the bait in the water. When fish are fussy, this subtle change makes a difference in your success rate and also alters the action. Always fix knot positioning on horizontal jigs. Of course, if you happen to be catching fish with the knot moved forward or back on the line tie, stick with it. In general though, it's usually best to keep the knot in the center.

With ice jigs, use small hops and quivers to imitate the tiny forage of sunfish. Consider that various aquatic organisms swim differently, so you need a range of jig-pause sequences. Horizontal jigs are well suited for using micro-shaking moves. The center line tie serves as the balance point. When you quiver these jigs, they rock back and forth on this centre axis, creating an irresistible, life-like action that fools sunfish (as well as crappie and perch) into biting.

For vertical (i.e., tear drop) or 45- to 60-degree angle ice jigs, a sequence with short, springing hops, followed by a pause, is a good base rhythm. When this doesn't produce, sometimes less is best. A small lift of the rod and a very long lull with no movement might trigger hits. At times it can be difficult to hold a rod still enough when fish are really fussy. In this case, placing it on the top of a bucket, in a rod holder, or resting it on your knee will work. This long pause tactic has saved me on many sunfish outings during midwinter when the fishing was extremely tough. It's dynamite for fussy crappie as well.

Remember to try different jigging moves and different baits. Thinner jigs drop faster; wider ones flutter or wobble. When you catch a fish, note what you were doing and using (size, color, and profile), and then look for ways to refine your strategy to catch more. Be sure to experiment too with the amount of bait you're using and replenish it often. Colored bait can make a big difference when fish are finicky.

Don't neglect hook maintenance either when it comes to ice jigs and sunfish. Fussy sunfish will suck in a bait gently and dull hooks mean inferior sets and lost fish. It's amazing what can dull a thin hook: one of the most common culprits is banging or snagging a jig on the ice hole. Keep tabs on hook points and touch them up with a file. Bending the hook point out roughly ten degrees to widen the gap will also improve your ability to stick sunfish, as will using jigs featuring upturned hooks.

Binocular Blue Eyes »

Bluegills have binocular vision and can pick and choose what they eat. So highly detailed, natural-looking baits and light line are important.

Brian "Bro" Brosdahl, Ice Fishing Authority and Guide, MN

Youngsters, biting bluegills, and the comforts of a permanent shack are the ingredients to a perfect ice outing.
Photo: Noel Vick

Dropper Rigs

I wrote about using a dropper off of a spoon in Chapter 9 and dual jig droppers in the Crappie Chapter (10), but downsizing is sometimes what's needed for uber-fussy sunfish. Brian "Bro" Brosdahl has an assortment of dropper rig tactics sure to fool fussy sunfish, as well as crappie and perch. When faced with tough fishing conditions here are two dropper rigs to improve panfish catch rates.

The foundation of his vertical dropper set up is a Northland Bro Bug which is tied to a 2- to 3-pound test main line and tipped with either one or two wax worms or maggots. The Bro Bug features a collar between its large bug eyes and the hook eye. It's here he ties on a dropper line using an improved clinch knot. He likes a 4- to 6-inch dropper for more aggressive fish, and a 12-inch lead for neutral ones. At the tag end he'll tie on a tiny #16 to #20 fly hook tipped with one maggot.

For a parallel finesse line instead of a vertical one, Bro again begins his dropper using a horizontal ice jig, like a Bro Bug. Then he ties in a dropper line directly into the mainline using a dropper loop knot (see photos). One end of the loop knot is cut tight to the mainline, trimmed as needed, and again a tiny fly hook is attached and tipped with a maggot when fishing's tough. To keep the dropper hook straight out and point up, Bro uses an improved clinch knot for a standard fly hook and a snell knot for up- or down-eye fly hooks. The dropper line should be shorter than the distance between the loop knot and the ice jig or tangling becomes a problem. In areas where only one hook is permitted per line, substitute the ice jig with one or two split shot weights.

Swim or hop these rigs for a natural, life-like presentation. The weighted jig will move more than the unweighted hook, which will glide up and down with a fluid action. For his horizontal dropper, Bro notes he'll often set up an underwater camera in a down-view position. He'll

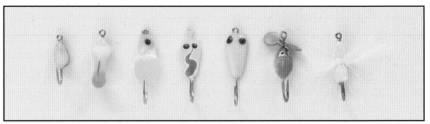

A variety of vertical ice jigs well-suited for fooling sunfish.

The dropper loop knot: 1) Make a loop in the line. 2) Spin the interior of the loop 5 - 8 times while holding corners. 3) Pass bottom loop through the top (smaller) loop. 4) Pull in all directions to tighten. 5) Clip the top of knot, trim as needed, and tie on a fly hook for horizontal dropper.

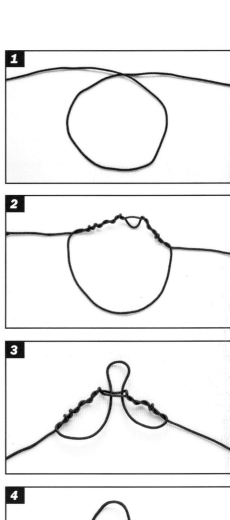

constantly hop the jig to imitate an aquatic insect and attract fish. When a bluegill comes in, he'll raise the dropper to the fish's level and then stop jigging. This often results in the natural twist in the line to unwind and spin the dropper towards the fish's mouth. Then he'll hop the set-up again to hold it in position in front of the fish and tease it to bite.

Another tip Bro shares is being aware of where your dropper is in relation to the weighted jig and watch your sonar accordingly. For example, if you spot a fish signal just below your jig on a vertical set up it's likely right on your dropper. Sometimes strikes are undetectable if a fish swims up with the bait, so he recommends slowly raising the offering. If the rod loads up, use a gentle pull and not a snapping hook set, as this will likely tear the hook out of the fish's mouth. Once you hook them, take your time because you only have so much flesh hooked on the fish and you can easily rip it out with too much pressure, he advises.

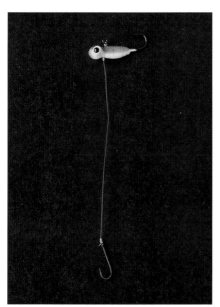

A Vertical Bro Dropper

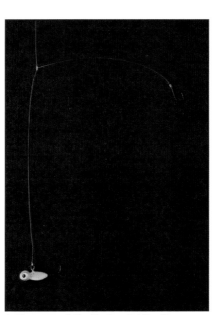

In the case of the Horizontal Bro Dropper, the dropper line is tied directly into the mainline using a dropper loop knot. Note the snelled fly hook.

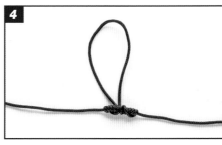

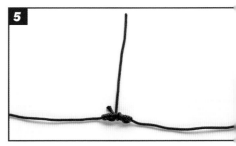

Pike

I recall when Jeff Gustafson first caught a glimpse of the northern pike pictured on the previous page. "It's a donkey! It's a really good one, boys," he shouted. Our fishing party gathered around and watched the battle as line came in and then slid back down the hole as the fish ran. When the northern was finally lifted out of the hole there was an on ice eruption. Hoots and hollers filled the air—even stealthy anglers get excited and break the no-noise rules now and then. Seeing this fish was one of many highlights of an incredible fishing trip on Lake of the Woods.

You have to respect the predatory instincts of northern pike. Whether you're battling a trophy or a smaller specimen, hooking a pike through the ice will have your reel's drag singing and get you grinning. Jigging and setlines both catch plenty of these toothy sport fish during winter.

SPECIES SUMMARY

Northern pike are considered a cool-water fish and regularly feed throughout the winter months, making them an excellent species to target beneath the ice. Pike are an elongated and slender fish with light spots set against a dark background of green, brown-green to almost a silver-blue. These fish have a long, wide head and a mouth lined with sharp teeth. Northerns are built for sprinting attacks and once they grasp prey, escape is virtually impossible.

Pike are not fussy eaters. The majority of their diet is fish, but they'll feast on whatever they can find. This includes frogs and crayfish. In open water, small rodents and ducklings also fall victim to pike.

Large, trophy-sized fish tend to be loners, but small- and average-sized pike will concentrate in areas with favorable habitat. So although they don't school, if you position yourself in a pike-friendly zone comprised of weeds or rocks and a decent forage base, odds are you'll catch more than one. This is especially true at late ice, when northerns of all sizes concentrate close to spawning grounds, although in some regions the season closes before this time.

FINDING PIKE BENEATH THE ICE

An adaptable species, pike live in a variety of habitats. At the start of the ice season, first-class areas on lakes are bays, humps, points, and around islands. Like many big predators, pike love edges, so factor drop offs into your search strategies. Finding the above structures near healthy vegetation doesn't hurt either, as pike are notorious weed line hunters. If the zones have the habitat to attract smaller fish (like perch) you can bet on pike being around. The same can be said for rivers. Bays, points, backwater areas, and side channels will attract pike throughout winter.

In midwinter, pike can still be found near the structures they're drawn to at early ice if forage is present, but deeper water is worth exploring too. In rocky lakes, fish also seek out deep-water structures like humps, points, and saddles. These locales are especially attractive when surrounded by baitfish, walleye, or whitefish. In fact, a selection of

Hot Pike Zones

A good habit is dropping a big dead bait below a tip-up while walleye fishing because pike share many of the same feeding locations. I've seen a really hot walleye bite totally shut down many times. Usually when this happens, the flags of the tip-ups start going off because a few big pike have moved into the area. Walleye don't like to hang out with big pike because northerns will eat them!

Jeff "Gussy" Gustafson, Professional Angler and Guide, ON

Davis Viehbeck with a pike taken from a drop off.

large pike will hold in deep water for most of the year following baitfish schools. It's not uncommon for anglers to hook trophy pike when targeting lake trout or walleye in baitfish-rich structure zones.

Late ice produces excellent pike fishing. Pike spawn following ice break up. Typical spawning areas are flooded marsh lands, tributaries, and bays. As the end of the ice season approaches, positioning yourself near these zones is sure to put you on sensational pike fishing, as fish are fairly concentrated. They're also feeding aggressively, dining on panfish and baitfish that have returned to the shallows.

JIGGING TACTICS FOR PIKE

Catching pike using stationary lines is very effective, but jigging can be good as well. Plus, it's fun to feel the aggressive hit of a pike on a jigging rod.

Large spoons, airplane jigs, and jigging minnows are all great choices. Use lighter spoons in shallow water and stick to heavier ones in deeper conditions. The flash and flutter of spoons mimic dying or injured baitfish. Rattle spoons are also deadly to attract pike and evoke vicious hits.

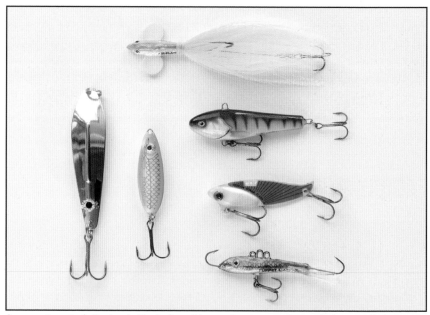

An assortment of jigging baits designed to create a commotion and pique a pike's interest. Left are a Williams Whitefish and a Northland Buck-Shot Rattle Spoon. The right row (top to bottom) are a Northland "Magnum" Air-Plane Jig, Salmo Chubby Darter, Heddon Sonar, and Northland Puppet Minnow. Note: these lures also work for lake trout.

The largest Northland, Rapala, and Nils Master jigging minnows are excellent choices as well. The swimming motion of these lures calls in fish by creating plenty of commotion. Plus, several consecutive rod lifts will get one of these baits dancing in a circle. This panic-mimicking move really drives aggressive pike wild, and they'll smack the bait in flight or as soon as it stops. For less active fish, try the passive jigging sequences I cover in the walleye chapter (Chapter 8).

Another popular pike bait is Northland's Airplane Jig. This offering is excellent when fish are neutral. Using lifts, slow falls, and long pauses is an effective way to work this lure through the water column.

You don't need to bait lures when pike are aggressive (such as at late ice) but it helps when fish are sluggish during midwinter. Apply the bait-tipping tactics outlined in the walleye chapter.

Be ready to set the hook at any time as northerns have no qualms chasing down a darting lure. Ultra-sharp hooks, stiff, powerful rods, and strong hook sets will land you more pike. Where it's legal to fish with more than one line, jigging lures in combination with setlines is a great tactic.

Pike Jigging Sticks

Because pike are built for powerful, sprinting moves, you need the right rod and reel combination for jigging. Overall, a heavy power rod is best to absorb the fight of a trophy fish. Longer rods of at least 32-inches are recommended to deliver enough force to drive hooks into a pike's boney mouth but also to provide plenty of leverage to move a big fish topside. When it comes to line, it's tough to beat 15- to 20-pound test superline. Just remember to attach a quality leader.

Tim Allard with a northern pike. Photo: In-Fisherman Magazine.

The mouth of a pike is all business.

SETLINE TACTICS

As fun as it is to hook a pike jigging, stationary lines are extremely effective for catching these toothy fish. Used exclusively or to compliment your jigging tactics, setlines allow you to fish a large area at a variety of depths for pike. Before getting into rigging details, it's worth spending a bit of time discussing tip-up strategies, since they're so fundamental to winter pike fishing.

Tip-Up Strategies

It's important to spread out baits because pike don't school but rather loosely group and hunt independently. Many states and provinces allow

Dave Bennett sets a tip-up quick-strike rig for pike.

for two or more lines per angler, so by setting up tip-ups with friends you can cover a large area.

Pike love edges so position baits along weed lines, above weed tops, or at sharp breaks between shallow and deep water. Also place tip-ups on travelling routes, like an underwater point, to intercept pike. Although they're fond of weed and structure perimeters, pike can be anywhere. So, to put it simply, set up lines in shallow and deep water, and everywhere in between.

For example, if fishing a large flat or bay, set at least one tip-up in the shallow area, at about 5 to 8 feet. Moving outwards, look for mid-depth areas to hold fish, such as weed edges, rockpiles, channels in the bottom, or the bay's entrance points. Common depths here could range from 8 to 14 feet. Lastly, probe the outer fringe of the area, setting lines at the top and at the base of the drop off into deep water, which could be 20 feet or more. Just be sure to cover as much prime water as possible. If you find that you're getting multiple fish from a certain depth, then adjust your other set-ups accordingly.

These suggestions apply to the placement of tip-ups over a specific fishing area, in this case a bay or slow tapering flat. Just as critical is the vertical presentation of baits. There's no magic recipe for where to set your tip-up minnows in the water column, but generally keep baits within a few feet of bottom. When working greenery, set the bait above the weed tops so pike can find it fast.

Tip-Up Rigging

I like underwater and polar tip-ups for pike fishing. Polar style models are excellent in freezing temperatures to help reduce hole freeze-over times. Big underwater tip-ups with large capacity spools are well designed for targeting deep water or trophy pike. Wind activated tip-ups are advantageous in mild conditions to give baits an added action to get a fish's attention. Just make sure you anchor the base down well and set the tension properly or a sprinting pike might pull it down the hole. Fill spools with 20- to 40-pound-test tip-up line. At the end of the main tip-up line attach your leader.

Pike tip-up bait is either a live or dead minnow. Evolution has designed pike to hone in on the flash and vibration sent off by a struggling fish, while a dead one is the easiest item for them to eat without wasting a lot of energy. Popular live bait choices include suckers and shiners. They also work well for dead bait, as do sardines and ciscoes.

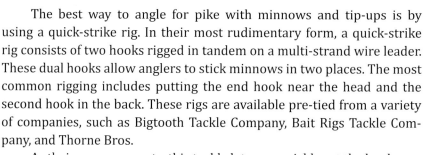

This photo illustrates the fish-catching power of an oversized deadbait and the gluttonous appetite of northern pike.

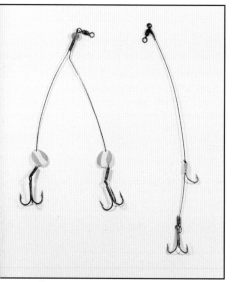

Here are two types of quick-strike rigs. The left model, by Bigtooth Tackle Company, is specifically designed to hold the bait in a natural, horizontal position.

The best way to angle for pike with minnows and tip-ups is by using a quick-strike rig. In their most rudimentary form, a quick-strike rig consists of two hooks rigged in tandem on a multi-strand wire leader. These dual hooks allow anglers to stick minnows in two places. The most common rigging includes putting the end hook near the head and the second hook in the back. These rigs are available pre-tied from a variety of companies, such as Bigtooth Tackle Company, Bait Rigs Tackle Company, and Thorne Bros.

As their name suggests, this tackle lets you quickly set the hook on a pike. When using single hooks, you must let the pike take the bait before setting the hook. But giving a pike too long to mouth and swallow a bait has resulted in the demise of many northerns who became gut-hooked. With quick-strike rigs, the waiting game is over. When a pike trips your tip-up, odds are they've grabbed at least one of the hooks and you can set immediately.

States and provinces have differing regulations on the number of hook points allowed per line when fishing. Adding spinner blades to quick-strike rigs classifies them as a lure in some instances, which usually allows for more hook points than a bare line alone. This might not always be the case though, so check your local ice fishing regulations carefully before using a quick-strike rig. If limited to one hook, many of the minnow rigging options outlined in the walleye chapter (Chapter 8) cross-over well for pike.

Tip-Up Battle Strategies

So, you've rigged your tip-ups and set your lines. You're looking over a frozen sea of snow and several lowered flags, when suddenly one pops up. Now what? Get over there and grab that line!

In the preceding chapters, I talked about the rush of fooling fickle fish, finding an eagerly biting school, or jigging-up trophies. But when you lock into a scrap with a decent northern on a tip-up, you enter another dimension of angling altogether. There's no sophisticated graphite blank to absorb the fight and dampen your mistakes either. It's just your skill and your gear against a mean, tooth-filled fish at the other end. This is angling reduced to its most basic elements and it's exciting.

Once the flag is tripped, hustle to the hole, raise the tip-up and set the hook with a long, upward pull of the line. Then fight the fish with a hand-over-hand approach to retrieve the line. When a fish runs, you'll need to let out line, so keep the area beside you as clean as possible. Clear away ice shards around the hole when setting your tip-up (a small shovel is great for this), to create an area for collecting line. Ideally, with a big fish, your partner will be helping to keep the line organized. Also place line downwind and use your body as a shield to prevent it from being blown around, which could lead to tangles.

As the pike draws close, look down the hole to ensure you leave a bit of depth between the bottom of the hole and the pike's position. You want to avoid pulling the fish to the underside of the ice from the side; this makes it difficult to maneuver the fish's head into the bottom of the hole. Instead, you're better off leading the fish upwards, rather than sideways, for the last few feet. Keep the pressure on the fish as it enters the hole, and it will naturally move upwards, ready to be landed.

Other Setlines

Although many anglers use tip-ups for stationary lines, you can also use rod and reel setlines too. Using quick-strike rigs on heavy power rods gives you the benefit of fighting pike with a pole. Secure the rod in a sturdy

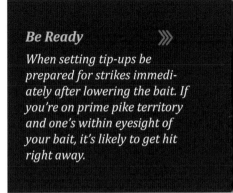

Be Ready »

When setting tip-ups be prepared for strikes immediately after lowering the bait. If you're on prime pike territory and one's within eyesight of your bait, it's likely to get hit right away.

A rod and reel setline, also known as a tip-down.

holder with a loose drag that lets line flow easily if a fish runs. Be sure to use some type of bite alarm (like clip on bells) to alert you to the strike.

Wrap Up

Targeting pike beneath the ice is big predator hunting. Rarely able to resist a wounded or dead baitfish, pike bite steadily throughout the ice season. As with most fish, midwinter can be a tough time, but overall, northern pike make for excellent hard-water quarry. This fish's drag-peeling fights, headshakes, and sheer tenacity makes it a great winter adversary.

Rob Jackson's a big fan of using tip-downs when targeting pike for the advantages a rod provides for hook sets and battles. Photo: Rob Jackson.

TROUT
RAINBOW, BROOK, AND BROWN

Rainbow, Brook, and Brown Trout

Trout ice fishing always gets me excited. It's a combination of the contest of catching them mixed with the possibility of harvesting a fish or two for a tasty meal at day's end. Of course, the serpentine squirm and fast runs of a hooked trout make for thrilling battles and trophies will test your skills to the limit.

SPECIES SUMMARY

Rainbow, brook, and brown trout are cold-water fish. If lakes provide cold, clean water and minimal competition for food from other predators, trout populations will often thrive. These fish live in rivers as well, but trout streams are fast-moving and safety becomes an issue as current makes ice thickness unpredictable.

All three fish have the typically elongated trout shape. Beyond that, their looks are distinct. Habitat, sex, and size for all species will affect their appearances.

Rainbow trout are predominantly silver. Their heads and backs range from dark blue-black to various greens, while their underbellies are light. The cheeks and sides of rainbows feature colors ranging from light pink to a dark red. Dark spots occur above the lateral line. Brown trout have coloration akin to their moniker: They're predominately a light brown with hints of silver and spots of black on their backs and sides, which may also have blue or red spot markings. Brook trout have dark green or brown backs that give way to lighter-colored sides, and a silver, white belly. Their backs feature light green or white worm-like markings, and their sides are dotted with red and blue spots.

Spawning times for these fish vary. Rainbows reproduce in spring, brook trout from late summer to autumn, and brown trout between fall and early winter.

Trout feed throughout the day, but action often comes in waves as pods of fish cruise through areas. Dusk and dawn, overcast conditions, and impending weather changes can also stimulate daytime activity. All

three trout thrive on a varied diet. Aquatic insects and invertebrates make up a significant portion of their food. Larger trout feed more heavily on fish (if available). This is why spoons and minnow setlines often catch the bigger ones, but don't discount the power of small baits to finesse large fish.

What are splake?

Splake are a cross between a lake trout and a brook trout. Due to their rapid growth rates, this hybrid is stocked in a variety of deep, cold lakes to create recreational angling opportunities. Their coloration is, as to be expected, a mix of their parents. In addition to the trout spots listed below, look for splake around moderate-to-deep structures like breaks, points, and reefs. Fish them with spoons, swimming lures, and plastic jigs.

FINDING RAINBOW, BROOK, AND BROWN TROUT BENEATH THE ICE

There are some general patterns that cover the majority of the ice fishing situations you'll likely face on lakes for these three species of trout. Beneath the ice, trout no longer need to retreat to deeper areas to access the cool water that suits their temperature preferences as they do in summer. Shallow areas provide them with the majority of their food and

Balls of Energy

Brook trout are not a slow-moving beast under the ice. They're actually very active and they move very quickly. I've seen some really big fish broken off because they're so powerful.

Gord Ellis, Outdoor Journalist and Professional Angler, ON

Rob Jackson with a splake taken from a rocky hump.

A rainbow trout taken from a small lake in late March.

comfortable temperatures at the same time.

Throughout winter, trout are attracted to bays, flats, and shorelines containing healthy weeds. Wood also makes excellent cover, and brook trout in particular have an affinity for timber. Lay downs and sunken logs will attract trout in surprisingly shallow water throughout the entire winter. Rocky points are other productive fishing areas. Muddy, shallow flats, bars, and bays will also appeal to trout.

During midwinter, trout will still often cruise through shallow cover and along shorelines to feed. If unsuccessful finding them in the above locations, consider moving to slightly deeper structures. One good option is to explore outside bends in a break line or rocky points. Mid-depth, soft bottom flats can also be good. These muddy zones will hold many aquatic insects and invertebrates that trout love. Midwinter is also when shorelines adjacent to deep water drop offs can be really productive, they're even better if lined with fallen trees or have rocky points.

At late ice, trout flood the shallows to feed. As plant life begins to grow under the ice, activity increases for many species and trout will chow down. Shallow weed and wood areas continue to appeal to trout, as do rock structures on shorelines, steep rock walls, boulder piles, and points.

Creek inlets and outlets are also popular trout zones, creating current and boosting oxygen. Finally, all trout species are drawn to underwater springs, which tend to concentrate fish year-round. Come winter, springs can reduce ice thickness or not allow any ice to form, so exercise caution: flowing water makes ice unpredictable.

JIGGING TACTICS FOR TROUT

Jigging catches plenty of trout. Many of the lures and tactics I discuss in the panfish chapters carry over well into trout-fishing, since trout also often rely on tiny underwater organisms as their main food source. Larger trout will take sizeable food items, but will still eat small morsels. Before exploring small ice jigs, however, let's cover spoons for bigger fish.

Spoons a-Plenty

Brookies, browns, and rainbows won't pass up a minnow as a meal. A spoon's flashy flutter mimics minnow distress, ringing an instinctual dinner bell for trout. In big trout territory (which can range from the Great Lakes to small, remote waters) spoons have a way of getting hits

Adam Howell with a brook trout caught from a shallow, mud flat.

TIPS FOR PRIME TROUT FISHING

Rainbow, brook, and brown trout are stocked throughout North America. Although many natural strains swim in our continent's waters, plenty of fish caught by anglers today are hatchery-reared. To put the odds in your favor of catching more trout, do a little homework before heading out on the ice.

Many state and provincial fisheries departments have stocking lists available to the public. Obtaining these lists is your first step to avoiding unproductive water and finding quality fishing areas. With the list in hand, review the historical stocking information; this gives an indication of whether lakes likely hold decent populations of trout. In many instances, stocking occurs either every year or every other year, so don't discount a lake because of a one-year interruption. Shortlist lakes that have been stocked on a regular basis over the past several years.

Another major factor that has an impact on the quality of fishing is angling pressure. Lakes with drive-up road access are fished more frequently than those accessible only with an ATV, snow machine, or on foot. Using a back-roads map, determine which of your shortlisted lakes are off the beaten track. Venturing out to these areas often yields above-average catches, as well as the pleasures of solitude. This doesn't mean that you should discount drive-to lakes entirely, as some deliver excellent fishing, especially in remote towns. But overall, the easier the access, the tougher it is to find trophies.

Several winters ago my friends and I got a tip on a remote stocked brook trout lake. After some research, we circled the lake as a spot to try once the ice season arrived. Our angling informant had stretched the truth a little and what was supposed to be a one hour stroll through the bush, turned into a two hour epic quest. The lesson: even when using topographic maps it's difficult to estimate hike-in time and snow adds another factor to uneven terrain.

Luckily, we gave ourselves extra travel time and brought lots of water to stay hydrated. The walk was worth it though. We iced several respectable brookies and had the entire lake to ourselves. This adventure contrasted one of my rainbow trout trips of several years prior. Word got out on a drive-to stocked lake. We were the first ones to arrive at the destination but we were soon joined by several other teams of anglers. Gas augers ripped through the ice, dogs ran around the lake, and one group even had a radio playing. We caught fish, but it was tough. In most instances, a bit of grunt work to access a remote lake will pay back dividends when it comes to solitude and quality catches.

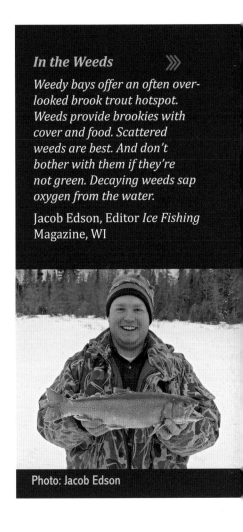

In the Weeds 》》》

Weedy bays offer an often over-looked brook trout hotspot. Weeds provide brookies with cover and food. Scattered weeds are best. And don't bother with them if they're not green. Decaying weeds sap oxygen from the water.

Jacob Edson, Editor *Ice Fishing Magazine*, WI

Photo: Jacob Edson

from aggressive fish. Popular trout spoons include the Northland Forage Minnow, Williams Wabler, Acme Little Cleo, Bay de Noc Vingla and Swedish Pimple, Hopkins Shorty, and Luhr Jensen Crippled Herring.

Standard spoon jigging sequences are best. Raises of 6- to 18-inches and freefall or controlled drops will call in fish. Sometimes, however, trout prefer short, snapping movements. As with other species, try a mix of jigging moves and register what produced a hit when it occurs. Then repeat the sequence again. If you need to finesse trout, jiggle the spoon with slight shakes of the rod. A word of advice: don't spend too much time trying to woo trout with delicate spoon-moves like you would for panfish. In my experience, if you can't get a trout you've marked on your sonar to hit your bait in a few seconds, they've lost interest and have likely moved on. Repeat your initial jigging sequence to call them back or attract others.

Baiting Spoons

Sweeten spoons with bait if possible, and rebait often so that they stay smelly—scent is often critical for trout to bite. A piece of minnow or night crawler will both deliver an appealing aroma. Artificial soft baits can be effective too. On small spoons, make sure tipping doesn't overshadow the lure's profile or interfere with its action.

Dropper Rigs

Spoon dropper rigs discussed in the perch chapter (Chapter 9) can also fool trout. Straight spoons rigged with short dropper lines tipped with ice jigs or even small, wet trout flies mimicking nymphs or fresh water shrimp, such as a Blue Fox Foxee Fly, can tempt fish into biting.

SUSPENDING TROUT AND SONAR

I fish all my trout baits though the entire water column because trout can be found at any depth. Sonar improves my catch rates, especially in moderate to deep water areas. Here's why: as groups of fish move through the area, they're often at different depths. A sonar let's you quickly adjust your lure position to intercept cruising fish.

On a small lake I fish for rainbows, one of my favorite spots is off a steep rock face point with a sharp drop-off into 18 feet of water. The sharp break funnels cruising trout. I'll mark trout anywhere from bottom to just beneath the ice. Watching my sonar for flickering fish signals, I regularly raise and lower my bait to try to catch them. I aim to keep my bait above the fish, because faint markings may actually be shallow fish on the edges of my cone angle (see Chapter 5 for a refresher on sonar cone angles and display interpretation). Plus, just as it does for any fish, the feedback from sonar helps me refine my presentation until I find out what trout are willing to bite on any given day.

Ice Jigs

Although spoons take big trout, small ice jigs produce consistent catches. I often start with spoons to gauge the mood of fish and see if aggressive trout are in the area. If I call fish in with a spoon but can't get a bite, then I switch to a dropper or ice jig.

These plastics are perfect trout hors d'oeuvres. Left row (top to bottom) Northland Mimic Minnow Fry, Bro's Bloodworm and Scud Bug, and Custom Jigs and Spins Ratso. Right row: Northland Slurpies Small Fry, Berkley PowerBait Atomic Tube, Exude Micro Crayfish and Nymph.

I use horizontal to vertical ice jigs as I would for crappie and perch and fish them with similar jigging moves (see Chapters 9-10 for a review of specific baits).

I'm also a fan of using small 1- to 2-inch tube jigs for trout, like the Berkley PowerBait Atomic Tube or the Northland Slurpies Small Fry. But tubes aren't the only micro plastic that catch trout. A variety of tiny baits are available that have tails that quiver with the slightest movement to imitate the underwater scurry of food. Good choices include: the Northland Bro's Bloodworm and Slug or Scud Bugs, Custom Jigs and Spins Ratso and Shrimpo, Munchies Tiny Tails, Exude Micro Crayfish and Exude Nymph. One- to two-inch twister tail grubs are another recommended trout bait. Some of these baits come pre-rigged, while others are best set up on small horizontal ice jigs or small 1/32- to 1/8-ounce ball head jigs.

A tube-fooled rainbow trout.

Jigs between 1/32- to 1/8-ounces tied with marabou and chenille are another effective trout presentation. When fish are fussy, these jigs can outperform others. There's something about a do-nothing approach or the faintest shake that makes these jigs come alive and be able to trigger bites. With the slightest movement, the hair or feathers wave and sway in the water in a natural dance, replicating the tails and appendages of aquatic nymphs that trout feed on.

Color Choices

Carry a mix of hot and natural colored lures and jigs for trout. Pink and chartreuse-colored baits are successful at times, but natural colors are often preferred. Flashy metallic spoons in silver, gold, and copper finishes work well. Accents of blue, green, chartreuse, pink, gold, red, and white can bolster a spoon's appeal. For ice jigs and plastics, carry a mix of natural tones like white, beige, brown, olive green, and black. I also like to carry glow-painted baits for low light conditions.

Top Trout Jigging Sticks

Use medium to light power rods with sensitive tips for jigging. Increased rod length gives added leverage for battling feisty trout, absorbs head-shakes, and buffers long runs, so consider 28-inches a starting point. Also be sure your rods are teamed with quality reels. Trout of any size will peel line during the fight and a big fish can snap it swiftly if your drag isn't up to snuff.

You'll want a range of line strengths for trout and you'll need to match your line to the size of trout you expect to find in the lake you're fishing. I use 4-pound test line the most. When in trophy waters though, spool up with 6- to 10-pound-test.

SETLINE TACTICS

As I've already noted, trout are cruisers, and so strategically placing set lines over prime areas will increase your catch rates. I've had my greatest success getting hits and hooking fish on dead-stick rods. The benefit of this tactic is that once you have a fish hooked, you're able to fight it with a rod and reel set-up, which is a big bonus when you get a trophy trout on.

>> *Trout Tips*

Trout aren't keen on noise, and if you expect to catch them, you need to learn to keep it low key on the ice. Refer to the stealth tips I cover in the sunfish chapter (Chapter 11) such as drilling your fishing holes well in advance of the prime time bite.

Trout are also notorious cruisers, so if you've positioned yourself on a decent flat or other structure on a small-sized lake, sometimes it's best to sit still and wait for them to move in. Fishing in a shelter to block out light tunneling down the hole is a good idea.

Minnows between 2- and 3-inches are perhaps the most popular setline bait for trout. Back or nose hook the minnow using the smallest octopus hook you can get away with, likely somewhere between a #8 and a #12. Pinch on a split shot anywhere from 6- to 12-inches above the hook. The further the weight, the more freedom the minnow has to swim. You can also use small jigs and the hooking tactics I described in the walleye chapter (Chapter 8). Don't forget to rebait minnows often to keep your offering appealing. On multiple occasions, I've had strikes within minutes of rebaiting my setline after lowering down the lively replacement.

Hard-core brook trout hunter and outdoor journalist Gord Ellis, of Thunder Bay, Ontario, has experimented with droppers on setlines. He'll use a 1/8-ounce jig tipped with a minnow or worm, then a foot and a half up he'll tie on a fly. "It gives them a choice and there are times they'll take one over the other for whatever reason.... sometimes the top hook snags on the bottom of the ice hole and you lose the fish, but those are the chances you take," he says.

Another deadly setline bait is a piece of worm on a small Aberdeen or bait keeper hook. Use a 1- to 2-inch section and thread it on the hook shank. Add a split shot to complete the offering. It's not a specialized configuration, but it catches fish as the worm imitates various trout edibles.

Secure your stick in a rod holder and loosen the drag. Trout hit and swim, so don't stray far from your rod. I've witnessed rods leaping from makeshift holders and sliding toward the hole before being intercepted by a sprinting angler with a dramatic finish much like a hockey goalie's glove save.

Tip-ups also catch trout, but if hits are light you may miss fish. You can bait tip-ups with any of the rigs described above.

Great Lakes Trout

The Great Lakes provide anglers with trout fishing opportunities in sheltered bays, harbors, and tributaries. Pat Kalmerton, of Wolf Pack Adventures has been fishing the edge of Lake Michigan near the Sheboygan River for 16 years. Before even talking about fishing tactics Kalmerton is adamant ice safety should always be a priority as changing winds and currents can quickly eat away at yesterday's safe ice on these massive waterways.

Drawing the Line »

My brook trout fishing is on the extreme side, so I tend to use 8- to 10-pound test when jigging. Generally if trout are going to bite, they're not that line shy.... Now, if you're fishing for brook trout that top out at 12-inches, you don't need 10-pound test. But a lot of the lakes I fish there's the potential to get four or five-pounders, and if you're fishing five feet of water that's loaded with a bunch of sticks, 4-pound-test isn't going to cut the mustard.

Gord Ellis, Outdoor Journalist and Professional Angler, ON

Photo: Gord Ellis

A setline worm rig.

His fishing is often a shallow-water approach in harbors averaging 6 feet, but he focuses on deeper holes and trenches around 8- to 10-feet created by a summer of boat traffic kicking up sand and silt. He'll occasionally fish up tributaries when ice is safe, looking for deep holes carved out by the flowing water on outside bends.

Kalmerton finds slightly deeper areas on otherwise uniform flats in harbors and bays are the hotspots, and where he focuses his jigging. He likes small two-inch tube, hair and tinsel jigs, or jigging minnows like the Northland Puppet Minnow. For setlines he uses a #16 gold treble hook tied below a small glow bead (for extra attraction) attached to 6- to 8-pound test fluorocarbon. "These brown trout are finicky and very sensitive, so light line and small trebles are a must," he says. Kalmerton uses the typical tail, back, or head hooking tactics I describe in the walleye chapter, but he also shares the following trick:

"When browns are aggressive and the water's murky, I often tail hook two minnows on opposite ends of the treble. When they swim they constantly fight against each other and this disturbance can really call in trout."

The Great Lakes can provide excellent trout fishing, and in addition to Kalmerton's tips, many of the tactics outlined in this chapter will work. Just don't under power your set-ups as trophies swim the waters of these iconic North American lakes.

Wrap Up

Elusive enough to intrigue winter angling fanatics and outstanding table fare, rainbow, brook, and brown trout are excellent ice fishing quarry. Their color markings make them beautiful fish to behold, but equally compelling is their never-give-up attitude once hooked. In the next chapter we look at another one of nature's cold-water bruisers, the lake trout.

LAKE TROUT

LAKE TROUT

I, like many ice anglers, hold lakers in particularly high regard, and for good reason. Hook a lake trout through the ice and you're in for a treat. Any size of laker makes for awesome ice fishing, but for adrenaline junkies the bigger the better. An average to trophy-sized laker will peel line off your reel and put powerful thumps in your jigging rod with such a violent, brute force that the event will leave any self-respecting angler awe-inspired and wanting more.

SPECIES SUMMARY

Make no mistake: lake trout are a cold-water species and active all winter. These fish are found in many parts of Canada and in the northern US. Lakers have an elongated shape. Their entire body has light dots and worm-like markings set against a light-to-dark gray, dark green, or brownish-black background, and their bellies are light in color.

Lake trout are rapacious predators, especially in cold water. Although trout feed on a range of items, fish are their favorite. Popular choices include ciscoes, smelt, perch, shiners, and whitefish.

Dave Bennett with a lake trout.

FINDING LAKE TROUT BENEATH THE ICE

Lake trout are found in deep, cold lakes. In summer, lakers are forced to inhabit deep waters that are cooler and more in line with their preferred temperature range. Once winter arrives, they're free to swim at any depth. Lakers are on the move frequently, either actively hunting baitfish or slowly roaming and looking for easy meals. When fishing for lake trout, it's critical to keep an open mind in terms of water depth. I've caught them incidentally while jigging a reef for walleye at dusk in 18 feet of water and also suspended halfway down over 90 feet.

When it comes to finding winter lake trout, studying a lake map should be the first stage of your search. Rocky outcroppings, such as humps, saddles, islands, and points, surrounded by deep water are prime zones. Focus on areas topping out between 25- and 60-feet deep. Steep breaks or bluff walls are also good spots. Lakers will use these natural walls to herd a school of baitfish into a no-exit zone and then attack, breaking it up and picking off isolated fish. Lakers sometimes also corral baitfish upwards pinning and attacking them against the ice. Having smelt swim up through the ice hole isn't uncommon when jigging for feeding trout. An inside corner is another laker ambush site.

"When I think of my top three best spots for lakers, they are all inside corners along shorelines. A description of this type of spot would be where a 15 foot bump sticks out from a shoreline with 60-plus feet of water all around it. If these bumps have an inside corner, where the 60 feet butts up against shore and the bump, you have a really high percentage spot," says ice guide Jeff "Gussy" Gustafson of Kenora, Ontario.

Large flats surrounded with deep water access are also good areas. Flats in the 20 to 45 feet depth range can hold a lot of forage for hunting lake trout, like whitefish, ciscoes, or yellow perch. Lakers move fast and can easily chase down prey, especially perch, on these vast, open areas with no places to hide.

Location Nuances: Finding Forage

Dialing-in lake trout whereabouts has a lot to do with finding schools of bait on good structures. A sonar unit helps you cover a lot of water and not waste time fishing unproductive areas that aren't holding baitfish.

To illustrate: there's a hump on a lake I regularly fish for lake trout and there are always smelt around it. The overall structure is roughly half the size of a football field and it has an inside bend to it. Feeding lake

Run-and-Gun Strategies »

Running-and-gunning is an open-water concept based on fishing fast and efficiently to cover a lot of water to find active fish. Nowhere is this approach more appropriate in ice fishing than when chasing lake trout. Lakers are cruisers and one of the best ways to boost your catch rates is to move a lot and drill plenty of holes. Find a good-looking structure, pepper the area with holes, and systematically jig the water column while watching a portable sonar for fish signals. Sometimes it pays to wait it out in a high-percentage spot that's produced fish consistently over the years, but generally, if you don't mark any trout on your electronics after working the entire structure, it's time to move to the next spot.

The author's father, Ray, with a lake trout taken off a hump.

Ever the entertainer on the ice, Steve Barnett tries a subconscious interrogation tactic on a smelt to extract information on the whereabouts of the lake trout.

trout herd pods of smelt (a main forage base of the lake) into the corner of the structure. Experience has taught me that locating the pods of bait with a sonar on this lake is critical to finding the position of lakers on this structure. The lesson? If you're not marking bait you're not in the zone and unlikely to catch fish. Moving around until you mark baitfish and then jigging is the best way to hook feeding lakers. We often drill dozens of holes over the entire area and then hop around to follow the bait and feeding trout. This is a prime example where team fishing with a friend or two makes you more efficient on the ice.

When jigging your lure among a school of smelt, using a sonar's important. You can see the large, strong trout signal moving through the smaller baitfish marks on the display and watch it rocket up to hit your bait. This helps you anticipate the strike and unleash a quality hook set. Another typical occurrence is the flickering bands of bait will suddenly scatter towards the bottom or off to the sides of your cone angle, clearing your sonar screen. When this happens, be ready. It often means a big laker is rapidly approaching. Keep jigging your lure at the same depth and hopefully you'll get a hit.

Of course, bait isn't the only factor to consider. I've been on lakes with such an overabundant population of smelt, that it seemed we marked these baitfish in almost every hole drilled over 30 feet of water. Here, bait takes a backseat to other factors, such as prime structure. On the other hand, I've fished lakes and barely marked any bait where we were fishing but managed to pluck trout during midwinter that were both suspended and cruising bottom in 80 feet of water. So, although bait is an extremely critical factor when hunting trout, it's not the be-all-and-end-all of laker location.

JIGGING TACTICS FOR LAKE TROUT

Given the lake trout's active winter disposition, most anglers prefer to jig for them and cover water in search of aggressive or feeding fish. Lake trout strikes can be crushing – putting a bend in your jigging stick that few other winter sport fish can equal. The good news is that a variety of jigging lures can take lake trout. Here's an overview of some time-honored lures and how to jig them.

Spoons

Spoons are a mainstay when it comes to ice fishing for lake trout, so a serious ice angler carries a wide assortment. From bent to straight models, popular lake trout spoons include the Northland Buck-Shot, Williams Whitefish and Wabler, Acme Kastmaster, Bass'n Bait Rattle Snakie, Deadly Dick Casting or Long Casting/ Jigging Lures, Luhr-Jensen Cast Champ or Crippled Herring, Bay de Noc Swedish Pimple, and Hopkins Smoothie and Shorty.

Having an assortment of spoons from 3/8- to 1-ounces gives you more options in lure actions but also sink rates. Bent spoons with plenty of flash are well suited to call in lake trout from a distance, but a straight, fast-sinking spoon with rattles might be the better option to get a laker's attention that's chasing baitifsh.

Carry a mix of spoon colors. Gold and silver serve as the foundation for most designs. Paint or prism tape in greens, blues, oranges, whites, and pinks are good additions. Natural forage patterns like shiners, smelt, rainbow, and perch are also excellent.

Tip spoons with a bit of minnow meat or scent-infused soft-bait. I've experimented between tipping spoons and not baiting them and noticed the difference can be substantial. A naked spoon can call lake trout in fast, but unless they're extremely aggressive, you might struggle to trigger them to hit. Adding some meat to the treble means that fish not only come in fast to the bait; they also crack it.

Jigging Minnows and Airplane Jigs

Both jigging minnows and airplane jigs deliver a similar circular, gliding action on the fall. Lake trout love this spiraling descent because it mimics a wounded or dying baitfish. It also offers an alternative action to the up-down motion of spoons. These baits work a large amount of water and help get the attention of nearby trout when you're jigging.

Large jigging minnows from companies like Northland, Rapala, and Nils Master will fool lakers. Natural minnow patterns as well as hot paint jobs both appeal to trout. Airplane jigs – like the Northland Magnum Air-Plane Jig – are often tied with hair. These fibers come alive under water and add a unique element to the artificial offering. Tip jigging minnows as discussed in the walleye chapter (Chapter 8), and airplane jigs by hooking

Finding baitfish, like the smelt pictured here, is an important step when looking for lake trout on the ice.

No Lazy Retrieves »

When bringing in your lure, always watch your electronics for new fish signals. The fast movement of retrieving the bait will sometimes trigger a fish that might have been out of your sonar cone. If the fish is chasing and you put on the brakes it's likely it'll smoke your lure, especially if it's a lake trout or big walleye. If you're bait's really high in the water column you can often hook them if you're able to drop it back down quickly enough while the fish is still hot and in the area.

Steve Barnett, Hard-Core Ice Angler, ON

a minnow through the head with the main hook and burying one of the trailer trebles in the back or tail.

Tube Jigs

I can't write about jigging for lake trout without mentioning tubes. These baits catch lots of lakers each winter and have an overall appeal that mixes profile and action unlike any other lure. The beauty of using tube jigs for lake trout is multi-faceted. A 3- to 4-inch tube jig has a likeness to several prey that trout eat. White, off-white, and pearl hues are excellent. In the deep, clear waters of trout lakes, these color patterns are quite visible underwater, especially on sunny days. Looking down an ice fishing hole, it's amazing how well a light-colored tube stands out. Lakers can easily spot these lures from a distance, making them effective when covering water and trying to locate active fish.

Tubes are potent for more reasons than just color options and shape. On slack line, tubes spiral downward, looking like an easy meal to lake trout. The spiraling also creates a lot of movement, making tubes useful to work the entire water column. Rig tubes on 1/4- to 1/2-ounce jig heads depending on the depth of water you're in and the action you're after. The lighter the weight, the slower the dive. When inserting a jig into a hollow-body tube, leaving space between the tube's nose and the top of the jig head causes the bait to glide more, boosting their spiraling appeal. An

The circular glide of a Northland Magnum Air-Plane Jig fooled this lake trout.

Photo: Topwater Media - Jeremy Smith

alternative rigging method is threading tubes on a jig head's hook shank.

Another advantage of tubes is that they have a great action when retrieved; they spiral or sway upwards with tentacles flaring. Reeling in the line and forcing an interested lake trout to chase the bait is a common tactic. If you can get a laker tracking the bait upwards, chances are that it will hit. Profile, color patterns, and a blend of attracting and triggering actions are the qualities that make tubes so effective for lake trout.

ICE ANGLING ESSENTIALS 》》》

LOCAL LURE PREFERENCES AND FISHING HABITS

Travelling to different bodies of water and fishing with other anglers in new waters is a highlight of being an outdoor journalist. Over the years, I've learned what the important questions are when heading out on a trip to a new place. One of these is if there are any specific lures I should bring. For the most part, I often have most of the baits the locals mention, but there's usually at least one lure or a specific color pattern I'm missing and need to purchase. In one place, I might hear, "You've got to have a half-and-half Williams Whitefish," or "Perch-pattern Buck-Shots are hot." Local anglers know their fish, and their advice is indispensable.

I raise this point in the lake trout chapter because sometimes having a lure that matches the profile and coloration of the predominant forage base in a lake is key to your success. On tough bites, mimicking their diet can tempt bites from snobbish lake trout.

I'm not advocating buying dozens of new lures every time you travel to a new lake, but be sure to pick up a sampling of the recommended baits. Don't assume either that you'll be able to buy them at your destination; hot lures can be tough to find once the season gets underway, especially in remote areas and on busy weekends.

With that said, avoid complete assimilation into local tactics when it comes to lures and fishing strategies. Yes, sometimes certain baits and presentations out-produce others, and if you're with a reputable guide, it pays to heed the advice offered, but your experiences will bring a different perspective to a water system. Consider local advice when it comes to lures, techniques, and suggested spots, but don't throw out what you know about ice fishing and your target species. Rather, combine regional know-how with your skills and experiences. Now that's a recipe for success on the ice.

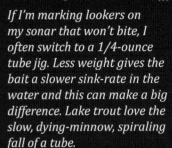

Slow Fall for Lakers 》》

If I'm marking lookers on my sonar that won't bite, I often switch to a 1/4-ounce tube jig. Less weight gives the bait a slower sink-rate in the water and this can make a big difference. Lake trout love the slow, dying-minnow, spiraling fall of a tube.

Dave Bennett, Fishing Guide, ON

Other Laker Baits

Blade baits are another type of lure that will take lakers because they put out loads of vibrations and flash. A major advantage to these lures is you can jig them fast and they still maintain their action. This helps when playing cat-and-mouse with a lake trout you've marked on the sonar. Popular blade baits include the Reef Runner Cicada or Heddon Sonar.

Bucktail jigs are also effective lures for trout. Tip the hook with minnow meat or a whole baitfish. Aggressively jigged, these baits do well for feeding lake trout. Minnow profiled plastics teamed with jig heads will also work.

Laker Jigging Tips

Jigging for lake trout runs the gamut when it comes to speed and moves. It's good practice to start by fishing fast for aggressive fish and then slow down if trout seem neutral. Mixing up jigging sequences with other fishing partners can help you figure out the mood of the fish faster than if you're solo. Quick lifts and falls with spoons, jigging minnows, and airplane and glider jigs work well. Raises of a foot or two and controlled or freefalling drops is also productive for most baits. As you'd expect, pauses will often trigger hits both on the drop, but also if you hold a bait still after raising it. Here are some other jigging tips to try when chasing lakers.

1. Short 6- to 10-inch snaps of the rod will get the attention of aggressive fish. Mix up the number and tempo of snaps with a brief pause. One of my favorite sequences is to snap twice as I raise my arm to lift the lure so that it jumps erratically twice as it swims upward, and then to lower it on a semi-taut line. This really gets spoons flashing and any internal rattles in a bait pumping out plenty of vibrations. This pattern is so effective at triggering reaction bites that my friend, Steve Barnett, who tipped me off to the tactic, has dubbed it "Jig, jig, whack," because aggressive lake trout will often hit immediately following the double-snap jigging move.

2. Another tactic is using quick, consecutive snaps so that the pattern is more of a snap-fall, snap-fall, snap-fall, pause and repeat. These fast moves aren't as effective for neutral lakers, but when you're trying to get the attention of fish gorging on schools of bait, they're pretty persuasive.

3. Although erratic jigging snaps have their place, sometimes less is best when lake trout fishing. "The biggest mistake anglers make when fishing lake trout is they jig way too fast and think they have to move the lure huge distances in the water. Lake trout jigging is a purely visual game when you use good sonar. Sometimes I hardly move my bait.... think of what you do for walleyes and do that for lake trout," says Gord Pyzer, Outdoor Journalist and Broadcaster from Kenora, Ontario. Shakes, short hops, and long pauses are productive subtle moves that fit into this toned-down jigging category.

4. Whether or not you use sonar when ice fishing, it pays to cover the entire water column when starting to search for lake trout. Begin by dropping the lure to the bottom. Lower the bait on a controlled line as lakers sometimes hit baits on the way down; this often happens if there are active fish in the immediate area. Once on bottom, jig the bait upwards in 10 foot intervals. Jig at a fixed depth for a minute or so and then reel up to the next depth level. Continue this method until you reach the surface. If you didn't get a bite and haven't marked a fish on your electronics, move to the next hole and repeat.

Steve Barnett with a "Jig-jig-whack" laker.

More on Sonar and Triggering Bites

Not to belabor the point, but using sonar will dramatically increase the number of lake trout you'll catch. These fish often move in and out quickly on baits and aren't likely to stick around too long if your jigging sequence isn't of interest to them. Sonar lets you experiment with different lure actions to try to get fish to bite. Triggering fish to hit is tricky at times. To start, keep doing whatever attracted the fish; sometimes this is enough to get them to bite. If this isn't successful, try to get the fish to chase the bait as the appearance of an escaping meal can convince a laker to eat. A word to the wise here: be careful not to jig your rod tip too high and keep it in the 9 to 10 o'clock range when teasing lakers to follow. If you get stuck with the pole in an 11 or 12 o'clock position or over your head when a fish hits, you've left yourself with no room to set the hook. Always keep yourself in hook-setting position.

Another benefit to using sonar is that as you catch and mark fish over the course of the day, you'll find a depth pattern where lakers are holding will emerge. Once you establish this zone, focus your efforts within its range. You can also use sonar to intercept a fish marked at a different depth than your bait. Whether they're below a ball of smelt or simply cruising suspended, dropping a lure down several feet above their location and jigging will catch fish.

Top Lake Trout Jigging Sticks

Lake trout will push your ice fishing gear to its threshold. Hard headshakes and fast runs strain your line, reel drag, and rod blank. Medium-heavy to heavy power rods between 36- to 46-inches are best for battling these cold-water thugs. Also opt for a fast or extra-fast action on a jigging rod. This stiffer blank gives you the power to play a big trout, but also reduces the effort needed to jig heavy laker baits.

Nylon and fluorocarbon lines between 8- and 12-pound test are options, but if in trophy territory go with 14- or 20-pound test superline attached to a swivel, and then a 1- to 2-foot fluorocarbon or mono leader. The no-stretch property of superline also improves deep-water hook sets.

SETLINE TACTICS

Jigging reigns supreme when running-and-gunning for lake trout. However, if staying put's the game-plan (such as when renting an ice house) a setline can land you a few extra fish. The tackle specifications and rigging

With the proper rod and reel outfit, Davis Viehbeck enjoys the sprinting runs and headshakes of a hooked lake trout.

techniques for lakers are similar to walleye and pike, but here are a few more tips.

Use heavy-duty tip-ups with large capacity spools for lakers. Stick with 30- to 40-pound test as the mainline and use a swivel to attach a 2- to 4-foot leader of 10- to 18-pound fluorocarbon or monofilament. To sink the rig, use a rubber core sinker or add an egg sinker to the mainline before tying on the swivel. For dead-sticks use the same set up as jigging. Secure the rod in a stout holder and back off the drag to prevent the combo from getting pulled free by a running trout. Attach a strike indicator (like clip-on bells) to alert you when a fish hits.

A stationary line rigged with a minnow placed a few feet off bottom will tempt trout cruising the floor, while positioning a bait midway down will catch suspending fish. Watch your sonar to see if lakers are swimming at specific depths and adjust rigs accordingly. Use a quick-strike rig or anchor a minnow in place on a jig. Try both live and dead bait.

Wrap Up

The cold-water biology of lake trout makes them an anomaly among most sport fish, in that they're quite active during winter. For anglers who get antsy sitting still or would rather power-fish than try to finesse bites, lakers are the perfect winter sport fish. Even so, lakers aren't the easiest to catch, and this raises the stakes and makes them a respectable opponent. Once you hook one, hold on. These fish put up some of the most impressive under-ice fights I've ever experienced.

WHITEFISH, EELPOUT, AND BASS

WHITEFISH, EELPOUT, AND BASS

In the preceding chapters, I discuss popular winter sport fish. These finned celebrities have the star power to draw in crowds of ice anglers and get a lot of press in fishing magazines and on TV shows. Yet there are other species that are fun to catch during the hard-water season. For a variety of reasons, the following fish are less targeted in winter and are simply not as en-vogue as the sport fish listed in the earlier chapters. Here are some other species that are deserving of more on-ice attention.

LAKE WHITEFISH

Often referred to simply as whitefish, this species is popular in specific regions and has been gaining a larger following among ice anglers over recent years. Widely distributed in much of Canada and select northern US states, this cold-water species is very active in winter and puts up impressive battles once hooked. Additionally, the delicate meat of whitefish rivals any freshwater species. Their coloration is predominantly silver, with light traces of yellow and brown mixed in depending on their habitat. Whitefish also feature a distinct overhanging snout. They eat an array of items including insect larvae, crustaceans, and small fish.

Finding Whitefish Beneath the Ice

Whitefish group in decent concentrations and can be found in a variety of areas in deep, natural lakes throughout winter. Whitefish spawn in the fall, often between November and December, but earlier in more northern lakes. Generally these fish spawn over rocky or sandy areas in less than 25 feet of water. This is important because early ice action is best focused close to this depth around reefs, bars, bays, points, and rocky flats. From midwinter to late ice, they'll often hold around deep structures like humps and flats in a range of depths. Thirty to 50 feet represents a suitable winter range, but I've taken whitefish out of 80 feet of water, so keep your reel spools filled and be prepared to fish deep.

Catching Whitefish

Chasing whitefish through the ice is a world of two extremes. You're either trapped in a game of finesse and subtle jigging moves with baits on bottom to attract neutral or inactive fish, or you're busy jigging lures for aggressive feeders throughout the water column. Let's look at these two scenarios in more detail.

Finessing whitefish calls for small ice jigs most often fished near or directly on bottom. Small plastic minnows and tubes around one to two inches or jigs packed with maggots or tipped with minnow tails are productive jigging baits.

Another style of lure popular for whitefish is in a category of its own. These front-heavy jigging minnows have a banana-shape, with the ends pointing down. There is a single hook at one end and a line tie in the middle of the jig. There are several models available, including the Blue Fox Lil'Foxee Jigging Minnow, Magz Manufacturing Badd Boyz, and Release-Me Baits Humpback Creeper. These baits feature a fast sink rate that's perfect for probing deep water for whites. Tipping the hook of these rigs is recommended. Good baits to add include Berkley Micro Power Nymph, the tentacles of a tube jig, or the forked tail of a small soft-

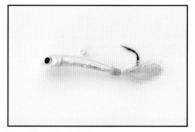

The Blue Fox Lil'Foxee Jigging Minnow is a unique and deadly whitefish presentation.

This whitefish was taken on a spreader rig. The wood is half of a balancing device that was set up inside a permanent shelter.

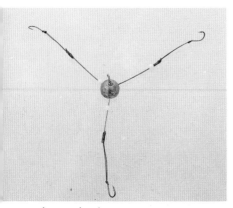

A spreader rig.

plastic minnow. Fish these baits with a quivering action and bang them on bottom to kick up sediment. Subtle nods of the rod cause the bait to rock slightly. This does an incredible job of mimicking a minnow feeding on the bottom.

Whitefish can also be aggressive predators willing to chase baits and when they strike, hits can be rod jarring. Overall, when you're in whitefish territory and fishing with a sonar, you can spot more active fish cruising the water column or hovering several feet off the lake bottom. These fish can be taken on spoons, jigging minnows, and plastic jigs in similar sizes as those used for perch or small walleye. I'll also carry slightly heavier ones, given the deeper water disposition of whitefish. Try using dropper lines beneath spoons as well. It's worth noting that whites have keen eyes and often display preferences for specific colors or profiles, so be sure to carry an array of baits. Some days, subtle differences can dramatically affect catch rates.

Present baits using light to medium-light power rods in the 28- to 36-inch range with 4- to 8-pound test line. For finesse fishing, spring bobbers can help signal faint hits. For deep water jigging, the stiff properties of fluorocarbon and no-stretch traits of superline teamed with a leader make these good choices for increased sensitivity.

Another popular presentation for whitefish is a spreader rig. These set-ups feature a heavy centre weight and then two to three hooks extending outwards on wire or stiff monofilament leads of several inches. Each hook is tipped with a small minnow, often through the back so they fight to turn upright. When lowered, the heavy sinker often buries in the mud and the minnows lie on the lake floor, struggling. These rigs can be fished from a rod, but many use this outfit on a secondary, stationary line. It's critical to keep a watchful eye on the rig and set the hook at the slightest movements, because wily whites can easily clean minnows off hooks without getting stuck. To boost your catch rates, opt for ultra-sharp hooks on spreader rigs.

EELPOUT

Eelpout have a cult following among ice anglers, which is evidenced by their varying aliases. Burbot, ling, freshwater cod, maria, and lawyer are common names you might hear. Some communities in Canada and the US hold festivals in winter where in addition to an eelpout fishing tournament, there are fish fries and other activities.

The author's father adds the final minnow to a spreader rig.

An eelpout - also known as: burbot, ling, freshwater cod, maria, and lawyer.

Eelpout are slithery and squirmy, here Rick Klatt gets a grip on one taken on a setline.

These fish are elongated and feature a chin barbel. They have long dorsal and anal fins with coloration ranging from dark to light, yellowish-brown. A dark worm-like pattern covers the top and sides of the fish, giving way to a white or light-colored belly.

Eelpout eat an array of prey, with fish being top choice on their menu. They are most active at night or in low-light conditions. This isn't to say you can't hook them during the day from deep water areas, however.

Finding Eelpout Beneath the Ice

It's not uncommon for lake trout or walleye anglers to hook eelpout incidentally as these fish are quite aggressive in winter and often share the same habitats of these other two species. Top spots include: deep shoals, flats, rocky reefs, points and humps. Eelpout hold in deeper, darker basin areas or flats found off these structures during the day, then they move up onto the structures at night to feed. These fish spawn beneath the ice and in surprisingly shallow water, sometimes less than five feet, on rock and sand covered bays and humps, so skinny-water catches will occur.

Catching Eelpout

These bottom-oriented fish are often taken on ice jigs and spoons tipped with bait, or minnows on setlines. The use of glow painted baits in greens, chartreuse, and yellows, as well as rattles, also helps fish hone-in on the

Time it Right »

Timing is the real key to eelpout success. The best fishing is usually at night, often past midnight. Also, eelpout are much more active and aggressive later in ice season. Which, coincidentally, is often when other species slip into the midwinter doldrums.

Jacob Edson, Editor Ice Fishing magazine, WI

offering at dark.

Eelpout put up hearty battles beneath the ice, so it's best to use a long, medium-light to medium power stick at a minimum. Go heavier if you're in big water areas where 'pout pushing 10 pounds are common. One last tip: eelpout are slithery, slimy creatures and have a tendency to try to tail-wrap your hand when you grab them. Hold them with care and be sure to carry a towel.

LARGEMOUTH AND SMALLMOUTH BASS

In many areas, the bass season is closed or limited during winter. Always be sure to check regulations carefully. When open, however, finding a concentration of smallmouth or largemouth bass often spells exciting ice fishing.

Largemouth and smallmouth bass are both warm-water fish making them less active than cold-water species come winter. This doesn't mean you can't catch them through the ice, though. Both species have an elongated sunfish shape. Largemouth are greenish-colored with a dark lateral line running down their side. Smallmouth are more brownish in color, with hues of golden brown to green depending on their habitat.

A subtle shake of the rod was all it took to convince this smallmouth to hit this Northland Puppet Minnow.

Finding Largemouth and Smallmouth Beneath the Ice

Look for largemouth at the start of the ice season around bays and shallow flats in lakes and backwater areas in rivers. Largies love weeds and if healthy vegetation exists, they'll be around it. Just as you'll find in open water fishing, largemouth seek out weed edges like those created by pockets or the weed wall where growth ends. They also love sunken wood. Timber-strewn bays and shorelines will hold bass, and if you find weeds surrounding timber, you've got an early ice hotspot. In midwinter, fish still hold in these areas, but as weeds die off they retreat to slightly deeper water. Late in the season they may return to the shallows. As weed growth returns in bays and along shallow shoreline areas, so do the largemouth.

When it comes to smallmouth haunts in the winter, the key feature is deep water. Autumn smallmouth bass angling can be incredible over deep structures, such as humps, saddles, and points. These locations will hold fish all winter. Smallmouth also have an affinity for rocks and hard-bottom areas, so factor this into your search strategy.

Catching Largemouth and Smallmouth Bass

Largemouth and smallmouth bass can be taken on a variety of lures through the ice. Ensure you drill plenty of holes – as bass are less apt to chase baits in cold water – but once you find them, you'll often get several out of the area. Again, using a sonar and adjusting your jigging moves based on the display's data is key to triggering bites from any species, and bass are no different.

Jigging spoons and jigging minnows are popular for both species. Small ice jigs tipped with plastic tails or maggots are good to finesse bass. I've been surprised on multiple occasions when targeting panfish in shallow weed areas and a largemouth hits the micro bait. A slight tick in the line signals a hit, but once I set the hook and feel the weight, it quickly becomes apparent that a bass is on the other end. Long, medium to light power rods and 4- to 6-pound test line work best for both bass species.

Photo: In-Fisherman Magazine

Wrap Up

Species like walleye, perch, crappie, pike, and lake trout get a lot of attention when it comes to ice fishing. These A-List superstars are popular for good reason, but there's plenty of hidden talent beneath the ice. Perhaps even better, though, is that with so many ice anglers flocking after the more sought-out sport fish, fewer folks are inclined to target the species I've discussed in this chapter. Meaning that there's less competition and better chances of consistent and quality angling.

SELECTIVE HARVEST TIPS

SELECTIVE HARVEST TIPS

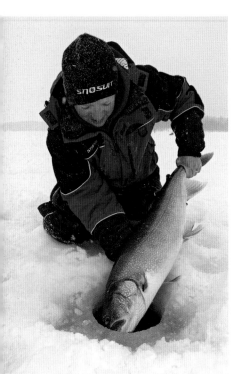

Catch and release and proper handling methods are critical to preserving fisheries. Here Davis Viehbeck carefully slides a lake trout back to its domain.

Throughout this book I've been touting the tastiness of various species and it's tough to beat a helping of fresh fish. But in order for future generations to enjoy nature's bounty, today's increasingly skilled and sophisticated anglers are ethically obliged to make conscious and informed decisions on the size, species, and numbers of fish they choose to harvest. This concept of "selective harvest" will play a key role in ensuring the future of quality angling opportunities. In this chapter, I'll review the concept of selective harvest, and provide ice fishing specific tips for catch and release, as well as suggestions on caring for the fish you choose to keep.

SELECTIVE HARVEST

Ice angling can put a lot of pressure on a fishery. In winter, many species congregate in high numbers at specific areas and ice anglers armed with the right tools and know-how can catch plenty of fish in a day. Although there's nothing wrong with keeping fish for the table, a bit of informed discretion goes a long way when it comes to preserving our fisheries and preventing overharvesting.

The concept of selective harvest is an important one. It's the practice of an angler making harvest decisions with the multi-faceted objective of both putting food on the table and ensuring the long-term preservation of the fishery.

In many cases, selective harvest is about releasing the largest specimens captured and choosing to harvest the smaller, more abundant individuals within a population. This is done in hopes that the larger released individuals may pass on their big-fish genes to future generations.

In other cases, selective harvest is about an angler choosing to focus their harvest on a locally underutilized or more abundant species (perhaps sunfish or eelpout) within a lake or river instead of adding additional harvest pressure on more commonly kept and less abundant species, such as walleye or lake trout.

It also includes considering the body of water that you're fishing and acting accordingly. When angling highly pressured systems, opt to not harvest any fish or reduce the amount of fish you keep to one or two instead of the full limit.

When deciding whether to harvest fish, your assessment should also be based on the number of days you angle and keep fish. One angler who only gets out a few times a winter and takes home the full limit will have a smaller impact on a fishery than another who gets out several times a week and frequently keeps a fish or two each outing. It's key to factor in the number of fish you keep per water system over the course of the entire year.

As anglers and conservationists, we all have a responsibility to consider this important concept when we are deciding which, if any, fish we take home with us; the future of fishing depends on it.

CATCH AND RELEASE TIPS

The selective harvest concept is intertwined with catch and release fishing. The goal here is to minimize stress to the fish during angling, handling, and release, so it can swim away healthy and survive when you choose not to harvest it. Here are some catch and release guidelines.

Always use the best gear for the fish you're targeting (in terms of rod power and line strength) so that you can play and land the fish as quickly as possible. Long fights that exhaust fish increase their recovery time. Also, minimize your handling of the fish and learn the proper way to hold different species.

For small fish, like bluegills, palming them provides a reasonable grip for removing hooks. For perch, crappie, and bass simply use your thumb to grab the lower lip. Use a gill-cover hold for small pike and walleye, lightly pinching their gill flaps with your index finger and thumb. For large pike, trout, and walleye slide your first two fingers inside the gill flap and then lock the grip with your thumb. What's significant with this hold is making sure you only touch the gill flap and not the fragile gills. Also, grab fish with wet hands whenever possible. Handling fish with gloves or dry hands can remove protective slime, which is their defense barrier against infection. To reduce the chill, keep a hand towel in a pocket or in your shack to dry off after handling fish.

Winter adds another level of challenge to the general principles of

Practice selective harvest whenever keeping a few fish for a meal.

Let the Big Ones Go »

The difference between a ¾-pound and a 1-pound sunfish is only a fork full on your plate, but it makes all the difference to the lake, so eat the smaller fish and let the big ones go.

Paul Nelson, Ice Fishing Guide, MN

catch and release. Sub-zero wind chill conditions can quickly start freezing fish when they are exposed to the elements, so act fast to remove hooks and get them back down the hole if you don't intend to keep them. For small fish, consider leaving them in the water while you remove the hook. They'll often do a 180-degree turn and swim back to bottom.

Inside a shelter or on mild days, you have more time to unhook fish. While you need to act fast, you also need to remember not to rush the release so you don't risk injuring the fish in the process. It's a careful balance between speed and care. Reducing air exposure is also necessary as fish can't breathe out of water. Having hook removal tools, such as a pair of forceps or pliers, on you at all times will speed up your release times. Also consider using barbless or semi-barbless hooks to make quick work of hook removal. Overall the good news is that, generally speaking, fish have better survival rates after being released into cold-water than compared to warm-water periods.

CARING FOR YOUR CATCH

The biggest challenge when it comes to caring for your catch when ice fishing is preventing freezing, which can damage meat and make cleaning a messier endeavor once home. Granted, sometimes freezing is inevitable but often keeping fish inside a heated portable shelter will help prevent the frost from settling into the flesh.

When you decide to harvest a fish dispatch it with a swift blow to the top of the head using a blunt object and keep it cool, again avoid freezing whenever possible. Also don't let fish bang around during moves as this will bruise the flesh. Buckets make great containers to transport fish. Once home, clean fish right away.

It's best to eat fish within one to two days of harvest, storing them in a sealed container in your refrigerator. If you can't enjoy your catch within this time-frame, freeze fish to prevent spoilage. There are plenty of opinions out there on the best way to prepare fish for the freezer. Proponents of all methods agree that ultimately air exposure is the worst enemy since it leads to freezer burn and degrades meat quality.

I've come across several different methods to freeze fish that work for me. One method is to freeze fish in water for added protection from air exposure in plastic containers, milk cartons, or sealable plastic bags. Alternatively, some anglers don't use water, but wrap fish multiple times in cling wrap. Using thick milk bags or vacuum sealed plastic are two other

A goodbye splash from a trophy walleye returned to its icy domain.

options. The key for all of these approaches is eliminating as much air as possible between the fish and the plastic. When you're ready to enjoy your frozen fish, remove it from the freezer the day before and place it in a container in the fridge to thaw.

Rob Jackson releases a jumbo perch.

CLOSING THOUGHTS

Nothing compares to time on the water – the best way to become a better angler is to get out there and do it. Keep a log of your adventures to record your good days and bad, and learn from them. Don't be afraid to experiment too, some of my most memorable catches have been the result of going against the grain.

Fishing hard and landing a lot of fish is rewarding, but remember the most important goal of all: having fun and enjoying time outdoors with good company. I get just as excited when one of my family or friends catches a big fish as when I hook one myself. Fishing-induced smiles tend to be contagious.

Catching fish and camaraderie are unquestionably core ingredients to a good day on the ice, but equally captivating are the stunning landscapes and wildlife that often accompany winter adventures. Don't forget to look up from your ice hole and soak in the scenery now and then.

Remember too that ice is the great equalizer. As long as it's a safe thickness, the freedom to explore is boundless. So grab your auger, safety equipment, shelter and other gear, embrace the adventure of ice fishing and plot your own course to success this winter.

I hope this book helps you catch more fish for many winters to come. But you're not going to hook anything unless you're on the ice. So here's the exciting part - it's time to go fishing!

THE **HELICONIA PRESS**

For more great books and DVDs on a variety of outdoor activities,
visit *The Heliconia Press* online.
www.helipress.com